"What a great book! I strongly recommend it."

—from the foreword by **Brother Andrew**, founder, Open Doors; author, *God's Smuggler*

"This is such an important book! Five words come to mind: *Important. Urgent. Visionary. Relevant. Grace-awakened.* Please don't get one; get ten and get them into the hands of friends."

—**George Verwer**, founder, Operation Mobilization

"God's love triumphs over the fears of Islam! Joy Loewen effectively reveals the spiritual battle for the lives of Muslims and the power of God's love through His people to draw Muslims to salvation. I applaud Joy as she displays God's heart and instructs us in His love through her testimony in this challenging and compelling book."

—**Diane Moder**, Islamic Awareness and Education Director, Aglow International

"Riveting, with every page and story smelling of gun smoke and lavender. From story to story, Joy guides her women friends as they taste the salt and see the light of Christ. She also crams the book with practical illustrations. This book is more than delightful; it is a must-read for men as well as women. Why? If we fail to grasp the message of this book, we will never really understand Muslims or their culture. So whatever good books are on your reading list, move this one to the front. It will be worth it!"

—**Ed Hoskins**, M.D., Ph.D., author, *A Muslim's Heart*

"This is a must-read if you want to introduce your Muslim friends to Jesus. You will read it over and over because Joy Loewen not only includes fantastic how-to's from her experiences in Pakistan (where we were co-workers) and in reaching out to Muslim friends here in North America, but she shares personal stories of how God led her step by step. In my epilogue to Begum Bilquis Sheikh's story *I Dared to Call Him Father*, I emphasize how important it is to honor our Muslim friends. In this book Joy shows us how to *love* them into the Kingdom. Enjoy and learn!"

—**Synnove Mitchell**, long-time missionary to Pakistan

"This book shares the feelings of many Christian women who long to be understood by their Muslim friends. The book challenges the reader to take bold steps in humility to share Christ's love. Excellent material from a seasoned practitioner whose lifelong goal has been to bring the Gospel to Muslim women. I believe this book will revolutionize our approaches in reaching Muslim women with the genuine love of Christ."

—**Samuel Naaman**, D.Miss., Department of World Missions and Evangelism, Moody Bible Institute, Chicago

"There is nothing so compelling as a true story. Through the author's countless connections with Muslim women, the reader is given an insider's view both of the difficulty of Muslim women coming to faith in Christ and of their increasing responsiveness—especially as we in the West befriend them as Joy does."

—**David Lundy**, D.Min., international director,
Arab World Ministries

"Muslim women will shape the next generation of Muslims. Read this book and reach out and connect with one of them, and let her see the beauty of Jesus in you."

—**Nabeel T. Jabbour**, Th.D., author,
The Crescent through the Eyes of the Cross

Woman to Woman

Woman to Woman

Sharing Jesus with a Muslim Friend

Joy Loewen

a division of Baker Publishing Group
Grand Rapids, Michigan

Published by Chosen Books
A division of Baker Publishing Group
P.O. Box 6287, Grand Rapids, MI 49516-6287
www.chosenbooks.com

Printed in the United States of America

Library of Congress Cataloging-in-Publication Data
Loewen, Joy, 1952–
Woman to woman, sharing Jesus with a Muslim friend / Joy Loewen.
p. cm.
ISBN 978-0-8007-9483-5 (pbk.)
1. Missions to Muslims. 2. Women missionaries. 3. Muslim women—Religious life. 4. Loewen, Joy, 1952– I. Title.
BV2625.L64 2009
266.088′297082—dc22 2009030581

10 11 12 13 14 15 16 7 6 5 4 3 2 1

In keeping with biblical principles of creation stewardship, Baker Publishing Group advocates the responsible use of our natural resources. As a member of the Green Press Initiative, our company uses recycled paper when possible. The text paper of this book is comprised of 30% post-consumer waste.

Dedicated to my
Emergency Prayer Community,
which has stood by me
in the battles and victories
to see Muslim women come Home.

Contents

Foreword

There is no such thing as a clash of civilizations. Not even a clash of religions or of holy books. There is only fear, and this wonderful book deals with that subject eloquently.

The apostle John said perfect love casts out fear.

Joy Loewen deals with this very theme. Faith and fear do not live in the same heart . . . and yet Christians fear Islam, Muslims fear the judgment and we all fear each other and the future. Everything becomes black, and then, all of a sudden, here is *this* book.

Yes, there is definitely a way out. *The* Way.

Touching, spiritual, personal and, therefore, costly. I did not say there is no price to pay.

Please, read this book.

Then pray.

Then go and do the same. The harvest—a broken world, really—is all around you.

What a great book! I strongly recommend it.

Brother Andrew
founder, Open Doors; author,
God's Smuggler and others

Preface

Twenty years ago few Americans were aware of the presence of Muslims in our homeland, and even fewer were informed about Islam, the religion of Muslims. But 9/11 changed all that overnight. Suddenly the world was shaken by a group of people, relatively unknown, who flew airplanes into the Twin Towers that fateful morning, killing the pilots, the passengers and thousands of innocent people going about their work in the targeted buildings. All around the world the word *Muslim* became equated with terrorism.

I cried that day for a couple of reasons. First, I cried with you, my Christian reader, in deep sorrow for the people who had senselessly lost their innocent lives and for the suffering families left behind, grieved and bewildered, still trying to recover from the horror.

Second, I cried for the many Muslims with whom I had developed friendships by the time 9/11 occurred. I watched as one after another my Muslim women friends, who perceived they had become individually and collectively odious in the sight of non-Muslims, retreated in fear and shame. Some of them stayed indoors for a few weeks, not brave enough to face the outside world and its judgments against them. I even knew some who wanted to change their children's names. I tried to imagine being in their shoes. I tried to reassure them of my love for them and that I was not blaming them personally for a tragedy that did not come from their own hands. It hurt me to see them viewed as dangerous and despised people. My friends had done nothing wrong. They were not involved in the planning or execution of the attack. Their fault was simply that they were Muslims.

Since 9/11 the Church has been going through both a declension and an ascension in regard to Muslims. Although today we Christians are not as ignorant of Islam and its followers as we were twenty years ago, some of us have developed a growing fear of them. Some of this fear has been fueled by the media, who have rightfully and of necessity informed and warned of the radical, dangerous groups of Muslims but have not always given a balanced picture of moderate or secular Muslims. Consequently the perception that Muslims are terrorists, or at least dangerous and worthy of fear, has lodged in some Christians' hearts and minds. Some of us would even admit that we view Muslims as untrustworthy or even as our enemies. Because of this fear of Muslims, some Christians want to run away from them. We share the same homeland with millions of Muslims, but we do not feel at home with them.

Another part of the Church, however, has become motivated by a strong desire to see transformation, rather than polarization. Equipped with the compassion of Jesus Christ, they have ascended to the divine opportunity that they see before them. They know that fear and love cannot coexist, and they choose not to give in to fear but rather to reach out to a people who need the truth and love of Jesus. Convinced that Jesus, if He were walking on earth today, would feel at home with Muslims, this group of Christians has run toward them.

I wish to counteract the present fear and prejudice toward Muslims in our homeland by sharing my journey of learning to feel at home with them. My motivation to share the truths about Jesus Christ with Muslims springs forth from the knowledge that God loves Muslims and has given me His love for them. I want them to know His bountiful love for all human beings.

My story pertains mostly to my friendships with Muslim women. This book is written for the Christian woman who finds herself afraid of Muslim women but honestly desires to rise above her fear and learn how to love her Muslim neighbor or colleague and feel more at home with her.

My journey is best described by five general stages through which I have walked in order to feel at home with a Muslim woman:

Stage One: Although reluctant to voice it, I do not like her or am afraid of her and do not want much to do with her. I lack the love of Jesus for her.

Stage Two: I feel comfortable with her socially and understand her better culturally. I find myself really liking her.

Stage Three: I explain biblical truths to her, and she listens and responds. When she responds positively, a deeper level of feeling at home with her occurs.

Stage Four: Biblical truths are understood and accepted. We are at home with each other in the Kingdom. We become sisters in the family of Christ!

Stage Five: One day we will be together at home in heaven as sisters in the Lord. We will be at home with each other in the fullest sense. This is the ultimate goal of feeling "at home with Muslims."

I remember sitting with Safia in her tastefully decorated living room drinking tea and chatting about her job when she interrupted the conversation and asked me, "Joy, just exactly what do you do?" I had known Safia for fifteen years and had tried to explain that matter to her countless times, yet here she was asking me the same question again.

But this time I answered her differently. I simply said, "Safia, I help prepare people for the next life."

She was visibly taken aback with the strange answer. Even I was surprised at what had come out of my mouth! I explained, "Safia, this life is short. We need to be ready for the next life after we die. I try to help people understand how knowing Jesus Christ can effectively prepare them for the next life."

"Tell me: How do you do that, Joy?" She leaned forward, appearing interested. And so, perhaps for the tenth time, I proceeded to unfold the wonderful truths about Jesus Christ, or *Isa al Masih*, as He is referred to in the Qur'an, which could lead her to understand how she could be ready for our eternal home in heaven. I had felt culturally and socially comfortable with Safia for years, but now I was beginning to feel more at home with her on a deeper level as she desired to explore the answer to her question. I wait for the day when she will find Jesus to be her home and we will feel at home together in the Kingdom as sisters in Christ.

Praise God, an increasing number of Muslim women are discovering Jesus to be their true home and are finding their home in the Kingdom of God. I remember when Farzana tried to drive to my home for the first time. She never arrived. Returning to her house, she called me and apologized that she had followed my instructions, but then the road, which had been wide, became narrow. As that did not make sense to her, she had concluded the road could not be the one to my house. I told her that reminded me of Jesus' words: "You can enter God's Kingdom only through the narrow gate.

The highway to hell is broad, and its gate is wide for the many who choose that way. But the gateway to life is very narrow and the road is difficult, and only a few ever find it" (Matthew 7:13–14). The journey was not an easy or quick one, but Farzana has found the narrow road that leads to her home in heaven.

The names of the characters in this book have been changed, and in many cases the stories represent composites of Muslims based upon my friendships with them. While my experiences have been with both men and women, in this book I refer primarily to women and specifically those residing in North America. I use my experiences from the past thirty years to illustrate how the stages of feeling at home with Muslim women are fleshed out. As you read my stories you will learn facts about Islam and how to share the Gospel of Jesus Christ. It is not my intention to present an academic knowledge of Islam, but rather to help the reader gain a clearer understanding of what it looks like to share Jesus Christ with Muslim women in our homeland.

May you be encouraged and inspired to move from fear to love and compassion, so that you, too, can say without hesitancy, "I am at home with Muslims." It is possible.

Acknowledgments

My husband, Ed, has believed in me and encouraged me to write this book. I have been blessed by many of his excellent ideas when I have been stumped.

Friends who have encouraged, inspired, exhorted and given prayer support to bring this book to fruition are too numerous to list, but some stand out: Dave and Synnove Mitchell, Lindsay and Lois Ward, Erwin and Heather Dirks, Jane Petkau, Pastor Bruce Wilson, Joyce Wiebe and her late husband, Abe, and Dr. Don Little. Mom and Dad Modricker, although now in heaven, encouraged me, even as a young child, to write. Jane Campbell, you have been a patient and delightful person to work with. All of you at Baker Publishing Group have been a blessing to me. Charlene Hoskins, I love your analogy of "The King's Gift," and it became even more special to me after I met you. Thank you, all my sisters in Christ who have allowed your stories of redemption and transformation to be included in this book. I love each of you so much. It was a few of you, my Muslim friends, who urged me to write a book. One of you in particular even sensed God was telling you to urge me to write. It was because of your insistence that I began to write. I love you, dear friends.

Most of all, I want to acknowledge that the deepest source of inspiration has come from the Holy Spirit. I have been amazed at how He has awakened me often in the middle of the night to give me fresh ideas for this book. The process felt like I was white-water rafting, and I enjoyed every minute of the ride! It definitely was not a leisurely canoe trip. I hope you will be caught up in wonderment, as I was.

1

The Engagement Party

I opened the closet door and surveyed my casual clothes. "What should I wear to the party?" I groaned with indecisiveness. In an hour I would walk into a gathering of mostly Muslim women.

I had been invited to plenty of these engagement parties and knew what to expect. The women would be wearing their fancy gold jewelry. And lots of it, too. Not just any gold. Gold from the Emirates—Dubai to be exact. Dubai is the gold capital of the world, as I am reminded by my Muslim friends. They all would know if one's jewelry was not Dubai gold. Nothing else would measure up to that high quality. I thought of my friend Lulu, who loves the finer things and was drawn back to her part of the world, where some of the highest quality gold can be purchased.

I knew, too, that the women would smell like the perfume section of a department store, their various scents drifting through the air. My mind flitted to the time when Safina took me into her bedroom and proudly showed off her collection of twenty perfumes neatly arranged on a gold, shiny, mirrored tray—all from Dubai, of course. They were lardfree *halal* perfumes, which made them safe to use according to Islamic law. I had to sniff each one and decide which fragrance was my favorite. It was called *Heaven*. Safina then sprayed it on me lavishly.

As I deliberated what to wear, I could picture in my mind's eye the fancy embroidered Arab caftans and gorgeous silk *shalwar kameez* suits the women would be sporting. Sighing quietly, I once again was reminded how plain I was compared to these women. Nothing in my wardrobe was suitable for parties of this nature, and I felt a twinge of apprehension and embarrassment. I do not wear gold jewelry apart from my wedding rings, and I do not wear perfume. "It is amazing I am still invited to their parties," I chuckled to myself.

I thought of my Iranian friend, who smiled at me after I told her I do not dye my hair but wear it "au naturel." "You are free, Joy," she said enviously. "I am not there yet."

Looking over my wardrobe at that moment, I did not feel free. I imagined the women looking me over and whispering to each other, "What a plain-looking woman she is!" I knew their eyebrows would be plucked and formed just right, accentuating their beautiful dark eyes laden with shadow and liner—just like those pictures on couscous boxes. *They know how to highlight their eyes, that's for sure*, I thought to myself.

Then, realizing where my mind had wandered, I spoke firmly to myself. *Enough of this. I am not in a competition. I do not have to prove anything.*

I decided on the well-worn, black and gold, long velvet skirt and long-sleeved top. As I dressed I shored up my courage to drive over to the community hall. I prayed, "Oh, Lord, thank You so much for this wonderful opportunity to represent You before these Muslim women. Please help me to do it well. I really need You right now because I feel nervous. Help me not to feel alone. You said You would always be with me, and I need You right now. Please direct me to sit or talk with someone You have prepared."

My dear husband, Ed, gave me a reassuring hug and said comfortingly, "You'll be just fine, Joy. I will be praying for you." I felt alone as I walked out the door and got into the car. How I longed for a Christian friend to join me! I wondered if any other women from my culture would be present to alleviate my discomfort or awkwardness.

A Misfit at Home

Walking into the community hall that Saturday night, I did not expect to hear Christian worship music coming from a room off the entrance. *Hmm, what is that all about?* Sticking my head in the door, I surveyed fifty Christians engaged in a worship service. Did they have any idea that in the next room Muslim women would be having a party? They must have known, I decided, because when I visited the ladies' room I spotted Christian leaflets on each toilet tank. I knew they did not realize that Muslims consider a bathroom to be an unclean place for holy books and would consider putting those leaflets there a dishonorable act. I combed my hair, took a deep breath and walked into the party room.

It was a fashion show, just as I expected. Approximately two hundred women, lavishly dressed and happily chattering away in Arabic, Persian and Urdu, entered the community hall carrying large pans of fragrant meats and sweet dishes. I knew I was in for a delectable treat of Eastern cuisine. Scanning the room quickly, I realized I was the lone Caucasian woman. I braced myself and asked God to make me stand tall and royal like Queen Esther, whose name my parents had intentionally chosen for my middle name. As I prayed and viewed all this from the doorway, my nervousness fled and enjoyment rose within me.

The men quickly dropped off their women and scooted away. Once the men were gone and the door closed, some of the women removed their *hijab* head coverings, but others, always cautious and prepared for the unannounced arrival of a man at a party, kept their *hijabs* on. I was not sure what grabbed my attention first: the many colorful balloons or the array of head scarves. I observed brightly colored silk *hijabs*, some with satin ribbon, beaded or embroidered, and the white ones edged with delicate lace. A small group of conservative Muslim women wore their large black cloaks and black head scarves.

Suddenly a hush descended as an Arab woman stepped in front of the large crowd and recited some verses from the Qur'an to invite Allah's blessing upon the auspicious occasion. Then bang! The Arab music began to blast at full volume, and the belly dancing began. *Oh, my goodness!* I thought. *First a recitation from the Qur'an and then belly dancing? How can that be?* But the seemingly contradictory events did not appear to be any problem for the women. One Arab woman, the most talented of them all, began to display her seductive skills. I was intrigued by the way she gyrated her hips without moving the rest of her body. Many of the women, obviously delighted with a night out, tied long scarves around their hips to emphasize the difficult hip movements and joined the lead performer. They belly danced to loud Arab music for hours, seeming never to tire of the action or the racket of happy talking, while children skipped around merrily.

I really feel at home here among these lovely people, I mused. I knew I did not really belong, as we were not of the same spirit and faith, yet I felt at home in the sense that I and they have lived in the East, now share the same Western homeland and have experienced the same passages of womanhood. I was comfortable. *Is this how Jesus felt when He left heaven to live in our world and to identify with us?* I thought. *He went to a lot of parties, too. I wonder what those parties were like for Him. As He identified with another culture, did He remember who He was and where He came from? Did He ever feel confused with His identity or feel like a misfit?* I was sure of one thing: Jesus demonstrated that He was at home in a place far different from His home in heaven and among people who were not like the saints and angels of His heavenly home. He came and made His home among us. He moved in.

Jesus came and made His home among us. He moved in.

"My Parents Arranged This Marriage"

As I mused on how Jesus might have felt, my eyes caught sight of the bride sitting off to one side on a decorated chair, looking demure and beautiful but unmistakably sad. *Strange that the party is in her honor,* I thought, *but she does not seem to be receiving much attention.* She looked familiar, and I recalled meeting her a few months earlier.

I had been wandering around a low-income housing complex at dusk trying to find a woman's apartment and was about to give up when I decided I should knock on someone's door and ask if they knew where the woman lived. An Afghan woman, judging by her dress, came to the door. In typical Afghan hospitality the stranger invited me inside. She motioned for me to sit on the newly purchased red silk and wool carpet.

"Now we feel at home," the woman told me as she ran her hand over the intricate pattern of the carpet. "You know, we cannot feel at home until we sit on our carpets." She served me tea, pistachios and fruit. One by one her children shyly entered the room and politely introduced themselves. The eldest daughter, Sima, was attractive and seemed to be close to marrying age. And now to my surprise, here she was months later, sitting on the bridal chair. Since nobody was paying her much attention, I approached her.

"Remember me?" I asked. She nodded, her eyes looking downward. "Congratulations! You look beautiful. Who are you marrying?"

"Someone in Pakistan," she replied slowly and sadly.

"Are you happy about it?" I asked, concerned.

"No, but what can I do? My parents arranged this marriage. I have to go live in Pakistan." My heart went out to her. Fear and apprehension shadowed the bride's lovely face.

"Will you live with your in-laws or separately, Sima?" I inquired.

"I have to live with my in-laws," she answered dejectedly. She obviously dreaded what was awaiting her, knowing that a new bride often has to work hard to obey her mother-in-law's demands. "Pervez told me his mother comes first and I would just have to accept that." I had no adequate words for this young woman. I simply gave her a hug and continued with some small talk until another woman walked up to us.

At Home with Muslims

I noticed a group of Afghan women who were keeping to themselves. Dressed in extravagantly embroidered, sequined dresses that looked full and heavy, this group of women looked uninvolved in the party. An unmistakable look of sadness haunted their eyes. Had they lost husbands in the war? Or perhaps their husbands were still missing? I could only guess the trauma that followed them across the ocean, lying unforgotten and unhealed in their memories. Azizeh, one of my Afghan friends, had lost her husband at the hands of the Taliban and for years was unable to sleep soundly at night due to vivid memories of his suffering. I wondered if any of these women had the same struggle.

Slowly I moved closer to them and smiled. "Hi, my name is Joy. You look beautiful." I had learned a smile is the universal language. When a verbal language cannot be spoken well, a smile communicates many words.

Staring at me in disbelief, their faces suddenly broke out into smiles. I wondered who had last told them they were beautiful. Or perhaps no one had ever told them that before.

Women all over the room watched me as I moved around the room. Their eye communication was a language of its own, which they all seemed to understand. One woman I knew, Khurshid, gave me a slight nod and smile and then came over to say hello. Years before I had given Khurshid the book *I Dared to Call Him Father*, a thrilling true story of a noble Pakistani Muslim woman who had found Jesus as Savior. I had lost touch with Khurshid because she moved to another part of the city two weeks after receiving the book. I got the distinct impression that she wanted to talk with me but something held her back. She left quickly.

"Where do you think my home is?"

Women whispered to each other. One of them, deciding to check out the lone Caucasian among them, approached me and asked, "What do you do?"

"One of the things I do is help Fatima, over there, with conversational English," I answered, sweeping my hand toward my English student from Libya who had invited me to the party.

"Are you Canadian?" she pressed further.

"Yes, Canadian and American," I replied. "Actually, maybe you can tell me where my home is. I was born in Yemen; my early home was in Somalia; I went to elementary school in Ethiopia, high school in Kenya and college in the USA. I met my Canadian husband in college. He brought me to Canada. Then we moved to Pakistan, not too far from the Afghanistan border. After ten years there we moved back to Canada. Where do you think my home is?"

Surprised, she replied, "I guess Yemen. It is where you were born. Are you Muslim?"

"No," I replied. "I am a Christian. Actually, even though I have lived in many places, I like to say heaven is my real home."

She smiled at the strange answer. "What were you doing in Pakistan?" she asked in curiosity. "Were you with the embassy?"

"No, we were with the church at a mission hospital," I answered.

"Oh . . ." Uncertain of what to make of me, a Christian, at a Muslim party for women, her voice trailed off.

I feel at home with Muslims. But it was not always like that.

"I love Muslims. I enjoy being with you," I assured her.

Even I was surprised at the strength of my love and affection for Muslim people, many of whom have become my good friends. We speak different languages and have different customs and religions. Yet I feel at home with Muslims.

But it was not always like that.

2

Childhood Fears

"Step in there, John and Joy," Mom and Dad directed, grabbing our hands securely in theirs. My twin brother and I stepped obediently into the collapsible canvas container that was slung over the side of the cargo ship and then lowered onto a barge, taking us to land. Standing on the platform of that canvas container, unable to see outside or over the canvas, we clung to our parents, trusting our safe landing to them.

Twenty long years had passed in Yemen before my parents, Warren and Dorothy Modricker, received visas to enter Somalia. Set apart for God to pioneer the Gospel into this Muslim country for the first time in history, my parents stepped out in faith to move to this unfamiliar country and give the Somalis the Bible in their own language. Now with two-year-old twins in tow, they set foot for the first time in Mogadishu, the capital of that country, which today is considered one of the most dangerous cities in the world.

"Daddy, I am scared," I whimpered nearly every night. A timid child by nature, I would jump with fright at the slightest provocation. I remember one night screaming frantically, "Daddy, come! There's a scorpion on the floor!" My father came running, his soft heart always responding instantly like a fireman on duty.

"Joy-bells, it's just part of a balloon," he assured me. Daddy took me on his lap and tried to still my fluttering heart by diverting my active imagination with silly stories about a little boy made out of mud who got into all sorts of predicaments.

Fear and love cannot coexist.

The formidable-looking daggers many Somali men wore on their belts, approximately at the level of my eyes, scared me. The detestable, huge cockroaches and ever-present black ants that could bite ferociously terrified me. The Islamic clerics' daily calls to prayer that bellowed over loudspeakers and surrounded our house in all directions haunted me. I wondered why they spoke so loudly, forcefully ordering people to pray. No one else ever spoke to me like that. I grew frightened of God. I became aware of invisible powers, but I could not tell the difference between good powers from God or bad powers from Satan. The two were the same to me.

Because I felt so surrounded by danger on all sides in Somalia, it was difficult, if not impossible, for me to believe I was truly loved by my parents or friends. Fear has a way of distorting our perceptions of reality and blinding us, making it difficult to process situations with clear minds. Fear and love cannot coexist. As long as we are gripped by fear we are not free to fully feel loved or fully give love.

An Attack in the Desert

My father, however, thrived in such a volatile environment. A dauntless, pioneering spirit of breaking new ground for the Kingdom of God coursed through his veins. Spellbound and shaking like a leaf, my little heart fluttering, I listened to his stories of courage and victory.

"One night when I was traveling by train through the dark, hot Somali desert in Ethiopia, near the French Somaliland border, the train was derailed by one hundred and fifty wild, bloodthirsty Somalis from the Issa tribe who were armed with spears, guns and daggers! From midnight to dawn they attacked and looted the train, their guns firing. Finally I and all the other passengers were huddled in a bunch on the desert to await our fate. I knew that most people who fell into the hands of the treacherous Issa Somalis never lived to tell the story. Just this past year, for example, another train was attacked by the same people. The director of the French-Ethiopian Train Line was stabbed to death and mutilated beyond description. Two Roman Catholic nuns were sliced across the breasts but survived. I knew I could die at any moment.

"But God answered our prayer, and our lives were saved. The looters left at dawn, and I discovered that my footlocker had been cut open with Somali daggers and looted. Among the items missing was my Bible. A passenger later picked up my Bible and returned it to me. Thirty chapters were missing. This is probably the only Bible in the world that has been through an Issa tribe attack." Many years later Dad gave me his ripped Bible in which he had written the account of the train attack. (A more detailed version of the train attack by the Issa tribe is given in the book *The Hardest Place* by Hellen Miller [Guardian Books: Belleville, Ontario, Canada, 2006].)

While my father tried to instill faith and courage in us children, he instilled more fear than faith in me. As a child, the dangerous culture and erratic movement around me made me edgy with timidity. As a result, fear gripped my life.

Later in life I discovered that Muslim women fear many things, too. While I feared daggers especially, Muslim women particularly fear the evil eye. They believe that if someone is jealous of them or wishes to curse them, Satan can harm them through the power of someone's eye upon them.

While I feared daggers especially, Muslim women particularly fear the evil eye.

Only when Muslim women realize that God's holy, loving and powerful eye upon them is stronger than any evil eye do they become fully free from this fear. Like my sisters from Muslim backgrounds who have turned to Christ, I did not come to know that strong, protective love of God for many years.

Fear Grows

Sitting under Christian teaching from my parents and my missionary boarding schools, I slowly became aware of the afterlife. As my mind began to process biblical truths, I started to wonder if I would go to heaven when I died.

One of my favorite games was to play Sunday school. I would pretend to be the Bible teacher, and my playmates would gather around as my students. I would go so far as to cut out pictures and attach them to an improvised flannel board, while telling lavish stories about them. But one game time turned out differently. As I stood there with my flannel board, I suddenly wondered if I was actually a Christian.

Shortly after that incident I had a troubling dream. I was taken up in a cloud to heaven, but the cloud was not strong enough and I fell back to earth. I did not make it to heaven! I woke up distressed. I was so worried that I left my dormitory room in the middle of the night and knocked on the door of the principal's house. I simply told him I was not sure I was a Christian. It did not seem to make him angry that I had interrupted his sleep. He fetched his Bible and read John 1:12–13 to me: "But to all who believed him [Jesus Christ] and accepted him, he gave the right to become children of God. They are reborn—not with a physical birth resulting from human passion or plan, but a birth that comes from God." It was a reassuring and clarifying moment for me as I believed and accepted Jesus as my personal Savior. For the first time I fully understood that I needed the Savior, Jesus Christ, to forgive my sin and cleanse my heart, and I believed His promise to take me to heaven when I died. I processed these truths and believed the love of God as a fact, yet I still did not have much depth of understanding about the personalized love of God for me. I had become a child of God, but I did not know how deeply loved a child of God I was. While my fears regarding my eternal destiny were laid to rest, earthly fears were still present. Many years would pass before I would be free from them.

Diversions

It was no easy task for Mom and Dad to divert my attention from things that gripped me with fear. It took a lot of coaxing and distracting on their part. One of the most successful diversions was accompanying Daddy on the scooter to make the daily trip to the post office. I was captivated by the view of the Indian Ocean from the post office and loved seeing beyond the whitewashed buildings to the big ships far off in the deep, azure waters. While today those waters are full of lurking pirates and are considered the most dangerous waters in the world, the Somali coast of my childhood appeared friendly and inviting.

On Friday afternoons I could count on riding in the Land Rover to the pristine beach, where we were largely left alone.

What fun to build sand castles and discover shells washed up onto the sparkling sand! Still today I love to pick up one of those large shells I have saved from my childhood days and put it to my ear to listen to the illusion of ocean waves rising and falling. The distraction of the Somali beach would calm my fears for a while.

Most comforting of all were the times I would sit beside Fahima, one of our Somali maids, in our primitive kitchen as she cooked our dinners on the charcoal stove. The weather was hot, and the charcoal fire made the room even hotter and smoky. But I did not care. This was home for me, and I was in my favorite room because I could sit with one of my favorite people. We chatted about many things. I loved Fahima. When she called me *Farahea,* the Somali word for "Joy," I felt as if we were family. When John and I came home to Somalia for holidays from boarding school in Ethiopia and Kenya, I could hardly wait to run into Fahima's loving, brown arms. Those arms gave me a sense of love and safety.

My Life Turns Upside Down

I vividly remember one fateful day when my life turned upside down, and those arms became my desperate shelter. That day spiraled me deeper into my silent world of fear, and I largely refrained from talking about that day until I married years later.

Mom and Dad had left the house, saying they would be back in a short while. Suddenly John and I heard a loud banging on the front gate.

Omar, looking out of breath and wild-eyed, gave John and me a strict order: "Do not leave the house. Mr. Groves has been murdered, and his wife has been stabbed badly. The killer is running around somewhere."

He vanished from sight, leaving us alone and terrified. Would the killer come to our house? What did it mean to be murdered? Our ten-year-old minds could not make sense of Mr. Groves, a missionary colleague, being brutally murdered. We shuddered with fear. We thought of his children, our closest playmates. Up to that point in our young lives, we had not encountered death up close. John and I immediately began strategizing how to be safe from a murderer on the loose. The bathroom door had a lock, so we hid in the small cubicle of a room that held nothing but the open, smelly latrine. It seemed that we were in that room forever, and my legs grew tired and shaky. My heart pounded loudly and felt as if it were going to jump out of me.

"John," I whimpered after what seemed like an eternity in the bathroom. "What should we do? Where are Mom and Dad? Why haven't they returned?"

"Let's go look for them," John decided. Nervously we crept out of the bathroom, found our piggy banks and took out a few shillings. We walked out the front door and for the first time in our young lives flagged down a taxi to take us to the mission headquarters, having no idea how much money it would cost. We concluded that our parents would be there. As the taxi came to a halt, Fahima stepped out of it. She took us in her strong, loving arms and turned us around to go back inside. Mom and Dad had sent word for Fahima to go immediately to the house to be with us. They had not thought that Omar would arrive to deliver his message before Fahima arrived. She assured us that our parents were on their way and would arrive home shortly.

I was not the same girl after that frightening day. For years I had the same recurring nightmare in which I found myself running for safety and everyone was killed except me. I could not sleep alone. Each night my parents had to wheel my bed into their bedroom. "The Midnight Express," my dad called the nightly journey. Every night before lights were turned off I went through the ritual of checking under my bed and in my clothes cupboard. Our home resembled a jail, with its front door bolted and thick iron bars over the windows. Only after all were checked could I fall asleep in peace.

Everywhere I went my young eyes surveyed those daggers around the men's waists. My fear continued to grow.

Fear for Daddy

One day I caught sight of the fat book *Foxe's Book of Martyrs* on my father's bookshelf beside his desk. I was curious as to what a martyr was. I began paging through the book and was horrified at the drawings of torture. "Oh, no!" I shuddered. "What if something like that happened to Daddy?" Bigger than life in my child's mind, my father meant the world to me. Beside myself with fear and consternation, I approached him. "Daddy," I faltered, "I am so afraid you will be killed."

Pulling me to himself, he tried to reassure me. "Oh, Joybells," he said, "it would take only sixteen seconds to die," thinking that would lessen my fears. I tried to imagine how long sixteen seconds would be. I left my father's office speechless, fear now deeply lodged within my being. At a mere ten years old I made a big inner decision: I would protect my daddy from getting hurt. I would not let him get murdered.

> ***At ten years old I made a big inner decision: I would protect my daddy from getting hurt.***

Fear has a way of blinding us and causing us to generalize. One zealous fundamentalist had murdered my playmate's dad, creating in me a fear of all Muslims. Obsessive fear spread through my body like a poison, eventually taking control of me and making me a slave to it. Except for Fahima, whom I loved as if she were my mother, it was impossible for me to feel at home with Muslims.

3

Help Arrives

I first noticed the handsome young man on the second day of orientation at Moody Bible Institute in Chicago, Illinois. We struck up a friendship 39 years ago, which has grown sweeter and sweeter ever since.

Ed and I are from different backgrounds, to say the least. I could not fathom what it meant to grow up in a big family on a farm on the flat prairies of Canada. Everything Ed shared with me sounded as if it were from another planet. Grandparents, aunties, uncles and cousins all knew each other, and most lived in close proximity. I, on the other hand, hardly knew my extended family. I never heard Ed talk about anything dangerous or frightening happening to him, whereas my life up to that point had been terrifying for me and marked by near-constant danger. Ed made me feel safe and loved. His teasing nature and keen sense of humor made me laugh until I cried.

Three days before our wedding, Ed arrived from Canada, and my joy was unparalleled. No more long-distance relationship! It did not matter to me where we lived—just as long as we were together. The happiest moment of my life was when we were pronounced husband and wife by the minister in that small wedding in Wheaton, Illinois. My mother and father were not present to witness our union, as they were in Africa at the time of our wedding, but that did not lessen my joy.

Little did I know that God was sending me to Pakistan not only to serve him but also to begin healing my fearful heart and preparing me for a future ministry.

After our honeymoon to Niagara Falls, we made the long trip to the prairies of Canada to set up our first home together. Nothing is quite so satisfying as a couple's first home. I would look out the living room window every afternoon at 5:00 P.M., anticipating the arrival of my new husband, home from work. We did not have much in terms of material possessions, but we had each other. Unquestionably Ed brought a new stability into my life, which was a welcoming help to my insecure and fearful nature.

Crossing the Ocean

After one year we bid farewell to our honeymoon home and made our way back to Moody Bible Institute for Ed to complete his theological studies. While there, we heard various speakers share what God was doing around the world. Encouraged by a parachurch organization to consider joining their mission work in Pakistan, we took a step in obedience to God and agreed.

My fear of Muslims had been buried for some years, as I focused my attention on falling in love, getting married and becoming a wife and then a mother as we welcomed our sweet daughter, Christina, into our lives. All of these exciting chapters of my life had helped to suppress my fears and push them far back into my memories. Yet now here we were, headed toward the Muslim nation of Pakistan.

Little did I know that God was sending me to Pakistan not only to serve Him but also to begin healing my fearful heart and preparing me for a future ministry. You see, as far as we knew, Muslims lived across the ocean. We had not met a Muslim in North America before we left for Pakistan. Yet God took us to Pakistan to prepare us for a ministry in North America. Indeed, our journey to Pakistan would eventually lead us back to our homeland.

Ministry in Pakistan

When we arrived in Pakistan, our Christina was two years old, and our son, Jonny, was born there. Ed was first involved in overseeing the maintenance of the mission hospital and the missionary housing on the complex. Then he was put into hospital administration and also oversaw the evangelistic staff, later working alongside them. My primary job was to be a wife and mother, but as time permitted I became involved in the evangelistic work.

Mostly I preached in the large women's wards of the hospital. Most of the patients stayed in these big wards. Even relatives who stayed with patients day and night, not just during visiting hours as in the West, came into the big wards to hear the preaching. Later I would visit individually with female patients. I also cared for some abandoned babies, led Bible studies for Pakistani Christian women or taught Sunday school, but most of my work was evangelistic preaching in those women's wards.

It was this involvement in evangelistic preaching and visiting patients and relatives afterward that proved to be my training ground and preparation for future ministry. I am quite sure I was not an effective evangelist in those days, as I was learning the ropes. But it was an excellent "school" for me. I learned not from reading books or classes but from actual firsthand involvement.

Fears Begin to Surface

Two years after moving to Pakistan, some uncomfortable doubts and fears began to surface. I had no doubt that God loved the Pakistani Muslims among whom I was living, but something plagued me deep within my heart, and I could not share it with anyone. Eventually I divulged my agonizing secret to a senior colleague.

"I know God loves Pakistani Muslims, but I do not know that God loves me," I confessed, hardly able to speak the words. I saw the shock register on his face, and his reply devastated me, convincing me that I should never tell anyone my inner doubts and fears but pretend instead that everything was okay.

"I am sorry, but I cannot help you," was his reply. I walked out embarrassed and dejected.

Shortly after that encounter I contracted hepatitis and became bedridden for six weeks. The aloneness and utter quietness of those weeks brought forth bigger and bigger doubts. Troubling childhood memories began to surface and haunt me. God seemed far away and silent. *If a human being cannot help me, then how can God help me?* I thought.

I knew from Scripture that God is good and loving and was not punishing me with this illness. Yet countless Muslim women had relayed to me their belief that God was punishing them when they became sick or lost a baby or loved one. As I lay there in that bed I could identify with those beliefs. I could not make sense of my plight. Then toward the end of the six weeks I received a surprise visit. The Holy Spirit, our Comforter and Helper, came to me in the midst of my turmoil.

My Visitation

I lay in my bed that afternoon feeling abandoned and depressed. My preschool children had been sent to other homes to be cared for. Suddenly I heard an inaudible voice say gently, *Joy, I love you. I love you. I love you.*

The short message was repeated firmly but tenderly. Both the voice and the message were beautiful and captivated my attention, washing over me gently like a wave that grew bigger and stronger. Nobody had to convince me it was the voice of Jesus. I just knew. Those who belong to Him recognize His voice. He was coming to me in my great need to wipe away all my doubt and misgivings.

I understood. For the first time in my life I understood. God had removed my doubt to uncover a hidden treasure. I knew I was deeply loved by Jesus. I knew I was the apple of His eye. At last I had found the home I had been seeking my whole life. In John 14:23, Jesus says, "All who love me will do what I say. My Father will love them, and we will come and make our home with each of them." Up to that point my relationship with Jesus was maintained by obedience, but I had never felt we were much at home with each other. He was more a visitor or guest than my loving heavenly Father. Yet now I knew that God felt at home within my heart! And now that I had discovered I was

For the first time in my life I understood. God had removed my doubt to uncover a hidden treasure. I knew I was deeply loved by Jesus.

cherished by my Creator, He could begin working on other areas of my heart that needed healing, such as buried fears.

This visitation by the Holy Spirit was life altering for me. I would go so far as to say that my life could be categorized into two parts: before and after my visitation from the Holy Spirit where He told me He loved me. I became a different person. I got up out of that sick bed changed.

Up to that point my relationship with Jesus was maintained by obedience, but I had never felt we were much at home with each other.

But in addition to that, I believe that being around so many sick Muslims on the wards ripped open my heart with compassion. Fear of Muslims essentially vanished as I daily came face-to-face with suffering masses of people. Instead of seeing daggers as I had seen in Somalia, I now saw terrible physical, emotional and spiritual suffering. I saw them as desperate people. My fear of Muslims seemed to vanish when I saw their suffering.

My visitation from the Holy Spirit that life-altering day was a baptism of feeling and knowing that I am personally loved by God. That happened with a "bang." But over the years of experiencing the mass of suffering of the patients and their relatives, I received a baptism of compassion and love for Muslims. That did not happen with a "bang." It was a process that God worked in my heart during our time in Pakistan. Indeed, God was preparing me.

God's Redirection

Every few months Ed and I drove into the capital for shopping, and we would go to fast food restaurants for a taste of home. At these restaurants we often would see crowds of university students, and a strange stirring happened in both our hearts. We began to long to see these students reached with the Gospel. This longing grew quite strong, but we never once imagined God was redirecting us to work with Muslim university students, as that would be almost impossible to do in a Muslim country. Later, however, we discovered that it could be done in North America!

In our last year of ministry at the hospital Ed, with the full knowledge of the local police, led a group of four Pakistani Christians to distribute literature in a conservative fundamentalist area. But a riot was stirred up by Muslim religious leaders, and Ed and the other evangelists were arrested and taken to the district commissioner. Eventually they were freed, but God used this incident to redirect our vision to ministry in North America. We put all our belongings in storage, thinking we might return to Pakistan at some point, but three months later we received notice that a fire had destroyed our belongings. The only thing that survived was part of a singed notebook of personal prayers written by our ten-year-old daughter, which a missionary colleague had spotted on a sidewalk and sent to us. We knew then that God had closed that chapter of our lives.

God's redirection became clear. We first started working with Muslim graduate students in Canada, and then the ministry branched out to Muslim immigrants and then Muslim refugees. Twenty years later we now minister among all three groups.

"What Do You Do?"

Hassan, a Somali Muslim university professor, once asked me, "What do you do, Joy?"

"I am with the Church," I replied.

"Which church?" he pressed further.

"I do not work with any particular church, Hassan," I answered him, to which he commented, "Oh, the Church Without Borders, like Doctors Without Borders?"

"Yes, I guess you could call it something like that," I chuckled.

Indeed, it is an unusual calling God has placed on Ed's and my life, but it is one that is tender and precious to the heart of God. While we Christians tend to think of ministry to Muslims taking place overseas, a huge door is wide open to us right here in the West, and we need to recognize it and get involved in it. But first believers need to be equipped. This is the reason I have written this book.

4

First Encounters

The first Muslim woman I met in North America opened my eyes to the immense challenges I would have to overcome before I could be truly at home with Muslims. It was another step in my journey.

I was walking down the hall of a sprawling apartment complex when I ran into her. "Oh, hi there!" I dove in, excited to meet someone from the land where I had spent the past ten wonderful years. "You must be from Pakistan." I knew instantly from her clothing that she must be Pakistani and was probably a Muslim, since her *dupatta* scarf modestly covered her bosom.

She looked surprised. "How did you know I am from Pakistan?" she asked curiously.

"Well, I lived there for ten years, and I used to wear *shalwar kameez*, too," I replied. "I even wore a *chadar*," I added.

"Really?" she responded, hardly able to contain her surprise. "What were you doing there? Were you with the embassy?" Pleased to meet a Canadian who had lived in her country, the questions started tumbling out one after another. By that time, we had arrived at her suite, and she invited me to come in and chat some more. I accepted her kind offer.

"*Ap ka kya nam hai?*" I asked her.

She replied with a look of disbelief and wonder that I was speaking her language, Urdu. "Zarina. And what is your name?"

"Joy," I replied.

I was happy to meet someone from Pakistan, as I missed the land and people. After ten years in the "Land of the Pure," as the name signifies, my heart had become attached, and I welcomed a taste of Pakistan in my life. Seeing Zarina's *shalwar kameez* made me miss wearing the same fashion I had worn for ten years. I had grown to appreciate the traditional Pakistani outfit of loose pants and long tunics. They were much more comfortable than tight-fitting jeans. And the bright colors were lovely and feminine, not like the dull blacks, browns and grays of which we are so fond in the West.

Seated at the kitchen table, we looked each other over, still chatting away in the way women do when they first meet. I glanced around her living room. *Yes, she is a religious Muslim,* I surmised, judging by the huge picture of the Ka'aba that hung prominently on her living room wall. The cubic stone structure that stands covered by a black cloth in the Great Mosque in Mecca, Saudi Arabia, is considered the center of the Muslim world and a unifying focal point for Islamic worship, and it was obviously significant in Zarina's beliefs. In addition, over her couch hung a large golden frame with the names of Allah and Mohammed in Arabic calligraphy, and a miniature replica of a mosque sat on the shelf near the television.

Zarina immediately busied herself making sweet tea with plenty of milk and a taste of cardamom, which she served to me along with a spicy snack of dried chickpeas. It had been a while since I had sipped a cup of milky chai like that. I felt at home immediately.

"Why did you come to my building tonight?" she asked inquisitively.

"I come here often to help newcomers and international students with conversational English," I answered.

"Where do they come from?" she pressed.

"Most of them are from China, Poland or Russia."

We continued to talk for a while. Before I left, Zarina said slowly, "I just had surgery for cancer." She seemed to have a sudden need to tell someone who might care about her. Instantly I was reminded how Pakistanis in the mission hospital where we worked harbored a silent fear that their illnesses were punishments from God.

"Oh, Zarina, I am so sorry," I answered, trying to imagine what it must be like to suffer something as serious as cancer at such a young age.

"*Allah ki marzi* ('It is God's will')," she replied in a flat voice, giving me the common Muslim response to encountering personal tragedy.

The *Mattim*

A few weeks later the phone rang. Zarina's relative back home had died, and a *mattim*, the Pakistani cultural time of extending grief, would take place that evening at her apartment. I assured her I would come right over.

When I arrived at Zarina's apartment, I paused a moment before I knocked. I heard hushed voices coming from within, all speaking in Urdu. When the door opened I saw men's and women's shoes filling the entranceway. *Typical*, I thought. *When someone dies the whole Muslim community seems to appear, for they do not like for anyone to suffer alone.*

The men occupied the living room. They were still maintaining the segregation of men and women, as they did in Pakistan. I was ushered quickly into Zarina's bedroom, where the women were sprawled on the queen-sized bed and floor, looking somber. For a moment it seemed strange to be led into her bedroom. In the future, however, I would experience many evangelistic opportunities lounging comfortably on beds. I squeezed onto the bed among the group of women.

I noticed the women were engrossed in a game of some sort. *Strange,* I mused. *At a* mattim? The *mattims* I had attended had been quiet, somber times, except for the occasional lament. Showing sympathy means the community comes alongside the family in mourning and sits quietly with them. They feel no pressure to make small talk and are not afraid of silence. But this *mattim* was different. A ring on a string was being dangled over the open palms of women one at a time.

"What are you doing?" I asked.

Zarina answered, "We dangle the ring over our palms. Where it stops on your palm determines how many children you have, their gender, and how many more children you will have in the future." I chuckled naïvely to myself. *How ridiculous!* I thought. Observing my doubt, Zarina said, "Joy, hold out your hand and I will show you." Without thinking, I obliged.

Observing my doubt, Zarina said, "Joy, hold out your hand and I will show you." Without thinking, I obliged.

"You have one daughter and one son in that order, and you will not be having any more children," she said confidently. I was aghast. Not only was she right, but I had just participated in a form of fortunetelling. I was shaken and felt contaminated, wishing suddenly that I could run out of the room.

It was my first encounter with the occult arts, which I was soon to discover are popular among many Muslim women, although they perform them in secret. Muslims would agree that all kinds of fortunetelling are forbidden in Islam. In reality, however, many are drawn to the mystical arts.

I should have known better than to oblige Zarina that night, as I have a family history of dabbling in the occult. My grandfather, who was involved in hypnotism, became furious that his son embraced the Christian faith and once tried to get my father to recant his new faith in Jesus Christ under hypnotism. He was not successful. Grandfather underestimated the power that is in the name of Jesus Christ, to which my father adhered with his whole being. In addition, some of the women in my family line enjoyed occult pastimes such as telepathy, levitation, playing with Ouija boards and consulting with mediums. The fascination of using hidden powers had a magnetic pull for them. None of these things, however, had touched me personally, as my father did not want me to come under the influence of these relatives, and I had had little contact with them. Having had no experience in such occult activities, I realized that I had been unprepared for that night at the *mattim*. I felt uncomfortable and unclean before the Lord.

When I got home I cried and asked God to forgive me and to give me more discernment about such situations the next time. Deuteronomy 18:10–12, with which I was familiar, convicted me of God's requirement for His people to live holy and separated unto Him: "Do not let your people practice fortune-telling, or use sorcery, or interpret omens, or engage in witchcraft, or cast spells, or function as mediums or psychics, or call forth the spirits of the dead. Anyone who does these things is detestable to the LORD." I felt disgusted with myself.

Our Friendship Grows

A few weeks later I met with Zarina, who still was finding it difficult to accept the state of her health. Wanting her to find comfort, I handed her the book of Psalms. She looked it over cautiously and asked with a hint of suspicion in her voice, "Are you a Jew?" I knew she was searching for a box to put me in. It was important for Zarina to identify who I was in order to help her decide whether to move forward in friendship with me or not.

"No," I replied. "I am a Christian. We read the Psalms, too, which the prophet David wrote. I think you call Psalms the *Zabur*. We find comfort in them because he went through difficult times." She thanked me and put the book in her purse.

The next time I visited, Zarina wanted me to watch a documentary about the sexual abuse some members of the Church had committed among the aboriginals in northern Canada. She said, "I have watched this at least twenty times, Joy. You should watch it." I sensed she was containing herself politely and trying to be respectful, yet her voice expressed anger.

Feeling ashamed and embarrassed and wishing I could change the subject to avoid the discomfort of the moment, I said apologetically, "I am aware of what happened, Zarina. It is really sad, isn't it? I can understand why many have been so angry about it. Some serious wrongs and injustices were committed. Many people's lives were ruined or damaged. I am glad, at least, that our government has not put it all under the rug but has been willing to deal with it."

It was sad to witness how important that documentary was to Zarina. It fueled her belief that the West is Christian and these kinds of abuses are what Christian nations do. It was frustrating trying to explain we are not a Christian nation per se, and that our church and state are separate. This concept was difficult for Zarina to understand, since government and religion in the majority of Islamic nations merge.

I began to realize the many barriers, obstacles and offenses dividing Muslims and Christians that prevent us from feeling at home with each other. For Zarina, it was not the slaughters of the Crusades or the Muslim perspective of injustices endured by the Palestinians, or even their bitter anger over what Muslims perceive as American aggression in Islamic countries, but it was the harmful abuses that took place in the Church that angered her. It became apparent to me that Zarina believed Islamic domination of the world would bring peace and security. She loved expounding on the golden era of Islamic culture, which started in the ninth century and lasted until AD 1256. Considering her strong convictions, I wondered why she chose to live in the West rather than in the Islamic homeland of her childhood roots.

Considering her strong convictions, I wondered why she chose to live in the West rather than in the Islamic homeland of her childhood roots.

Listening to Zarina's anger and apologizing for the wrongs some Christians had done did seem to help. The adversarial air that was present at the beginning of our visit calmed, and we enjoyed the remainder of the evening.

Eid al Fitr

As her defenses came down, Zarina extended an invitation to the upcoming Muslim festival of *Eid al Fitr*, which ends the month of obligatory fasting. She was planning to put on a sumptuous *Eid* meal at her home.

"Would you like to come on Friday?" she inquired.

"Certainly. I would be honored. Thank you so much for inviting me," I replied. I quickly discovered that Muslim women are quite hospitable, and I would learn a lot from them in this area.

When the evening arrived I wrapped a candy dish gift to take with me and knocked on Zarina's door. A large group of Pakistani women dressed in beautiful new *shalwar kameez* outfits quieted and stared at me as I entered the room. As they eyed me suspiciously, I wondered if I could ever feel at home with them. Breaking the silence and thinking that I would not understand her native language, one of them asked Zarina in Urdu, "Is the English person a Muslim?" It was important to them to size me up religiously, a trait so unlike many Westerners who would put knowing one's religious affiliation at the bottom of the list.

"No, I am a Christian," I replied. It was their turn to be surprised. Yet my understanding what the woman had asked Zarina helped to quiet any remaining suspicions. Soon we were engaged in a lively conversation.

After the awkward beginning, I started to feel more at home among the Muslim women, even though it was not my religious holiday. They had just completed Ramadan, a month of fasting from dawn to dusk each day that is one of the principle tenets of Islam and unites all Muslims. During this time Muslims are aware of the need to cleanse their souls from mistakes made in the past year, and they believe they will receive extra blessings from Allah for fasting. They also believe that Satan retreats from them during this time. They fast during the daylight hours and in the evenings join with other families to enjoy special dishes together.

Manal, who was from Syria, explained to me how special keeping the fast was for her. Insensitively I joked that Muslims fast during the day and party at night. Manal was offended by my joking attitude. She felt I was being disrespectful, and she no longer felt at home with me. That was the last time I saw Manal. I have made numerous mistakes like that and regretted them later.

Zarina had prepared a large meal of *pulao* rice, chicken and lamb curries, sweet rice turned yellow by the exotic saffron spice, and a delicious *kheer* pudding sprinkled with ground pistachios, a favorite of mine. After a while, the women excused themselves one by one, as they had other homes to visit on *Eid*.

"Joy, I do not understand why I got cancer. I went on the Hajj *pilgrimage to Mecca twice." My heart went out to her.*

My belly full with the delicious Pakistani meal, I was preparing to leave as well, when Zarina took me aside and confided, "Joy, I do not understand why I got cancer. I went on the *Hajj* pilgrimage to Mecca twice." My heart went out to her.

Muslims make the pilgrimage to Mecca, Saudi Arabia, to fulfill their religious obligation. One thing they desire to do there is obtain Zamzam water, which is considered to have healing powers. According to Muslims, Zamzam is the name of the well from which Hagar and Ishmael drank when they were languishing in the desert. They believe Allah miraculously provided the water they needed. The version recorded in the Bible poignantly reveals that God heard Hagar's cry, saw their suffering and demonstrated that He truly cared for them. The conversation God had with Hagar is indeed precious, for He calls Hagar by name. Muslims like Zarina hope that a drink of that Zamzam water will heal them of their afflictions. Since Zarina had not obtained the healing she desired, she confided that she was planning another *Hajj* pilgrimage. She hoped that this time she would be made well, *inshallah* ("if Allah wills").

If Zarina only knew that she can find both healing and the Water of Life that quenches our spiritual thirst—right here in Canada, free of charge! I thought. I prayed that my friend would find her thirst quenched in Jesus Christ.

Many Firsts and Finding Common Beliefs

Those two first events with Zarina, the *mattim* and the *Eid* party, were full of firsts for me. These were the first Muslim women I had encountered in the West. Participating in the palm reading at the *mattim* was my first encounter with this kind of occult activity. Zarina gave me my first insight into how seriously some historical religious wrongs had affected my Muslim friends. For the first time I realized the almost impenetrable walls between Muslims and Christians. Learning about Zarina's trips to Mecca was another first encounter for me. So many firsts—I could hardly process them all. Where would I even begin sharing the Gospel? I felt overwhelmed. My head swirled with a sense of utter inadequacy and helplessness. *Maybe I am in over my head*, I thought.

In the midst of a deluge of challenges, I was relieved to find some common issues of faith that I could use as a bridge with Zarina. Early in our friendship she expressed curiosity about what our Bible says about Jesus Christ coming back at the end of the world, because her Islamic faith taught that, too. I soon discovered that this topic is of great interest to nearly every Muslim—man or woman, rich or poor, educated or illiterate.

One day stands out in particular. That morning I visited an illiterate Muslim friend, Faduma, who had lived in a small village in her homeland but now resided in North America. She was trying hard to catch up with modernity and learn the alphabet as an adult. We started talking about Jesus returning to earth, which led to an hour of my explaining from Scripture the signs that will precede His return and why He will return. She sat transfixed with all the information. "This has been an interesting conversation today!" Faduma exclaimed to me. "I like talking about these kinds of things."

In the afternoon another hour of animated conversation took place in a home owned by a wealthy, professional Muslim couple. I first read Revelation 1:7: "Look! He comes with the clouds of heaven. And everyone will see him—even those who pierced him. And all the nations of the world will mourn for him. Yes! Amen!" I then asked the couple if they understood why all the nations, including their Islamic country, will weep when they see Jesus Christ return. They looked puzzled and wanted to know what I thought, giving me a wonderful opportunity to explain how every person will recognize that Jesus is Lord and weep because they did not understand clearly, did not hear or did not believe the truth. I urged them to deal with Jesus now because at His Second Coming He will return as Savior and Judge. Finding common beliefs like the return of Christ helped me to weather the overwhelming challenges of witnessing to Muslims.

A Unique, God-given Opportunity

Zarina showed me numerous challenges and obstacles to feeling at home with her and other Muslim women I would meet. Only by coming to a better understanding of her and taking a humble stance would I ever be allowed to continue being welcomed into her life. Zarina made me face some issues I would rather have avoided and dismissed. I did not want to think about, least of all talk about, the obstacles created by the Crusades, Zionism, the Palestinian issue or Church abuses. It was all too complicated to sort out or fix. I was not sure if I was up to it. First encounters can be awkward, but we must not let that deter us from developing friendships. Rather than tackling the differences, we must try to find common ground.

While I met Zarina walking down the corridors of her apartment building, I have met others at university, at work or through tutoring English. But we also can encounter Muslims in our neighborhoods or at our children's schools.

Muslims are now residing in all major cities and even in rural areas in the West. Some of them have found Western nations to be safe refuges from the traumas of war and displacement. Those fleeing political and religious persecution are breathing new freedoms. Others, like Zarina, are equipped with professional skills and have immigrated with the dream of pursuing economic opportunities. And, of course, some Muslims have immigrated to the West to propagate Islam, as is evident on university campuses.

Muslim women in the West are not all the same. Zarina's Islamic worldview was political in nature. She passionately desired that Islam dominate the whole world and was zealous to participate in that goal. At the other end of the spectrum, the faith of some Muslim women is more cultural or secular in nature. They may fast and say their prescribed prayers but not wear the *hijab*. They easily syncretize their faith with other religious influences surrounding them. As they adapt and assimilate into Western culture, they may even adopt customs such as putting up a Christmas tree and having a gift exchange at Christmastime. Some Muslim women, too, are enclosed in traditionalism, combining religious beliefs with age-old customs and traditions that are carried down through the generations without much change. It is harder for them to adapt and assimilate into Western culture, for they are reluctant to adopt anything that may be equated with the "Christian West." On the other hand, Muslim women who have a faith that is more experiential than orthodox may have embraced the mystical tradition of Islam called Sufism. They are not as concerned about the letter of the law as they are with trying to connect with Allah in a personal way. It is important to recognize that Muslim women in the West are not all the same but reflect a mosaic of differences, especially in their dress, cuisine, languages and faith practices. All of them, however, adhere to three essential matters: a belief in Allah, the belief that Mohammed was the last messenger of Allah and a belief in their holy book, the Qur'an, even if they have not read it or lack knowledge about it.

As the Church of Jesus Christ, we can view the coming of Muslims to Western nations as a unique opportunity to befriend them and make Christ known. Most Muslims have not met a Christian in their Islamic countries, heard an explanation of salvation or visited a church. And now, in some divinely appointed way, God brings us together.

5

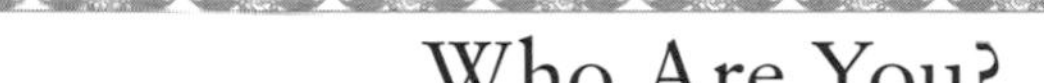

Who Are You?

Amal was confused. She was searching for a label to define me. "You *rahab*?" she asked in broken English.

Oh, my goodness! She thinks I am a prostitute! The word *rahab* was not familiar to me apart from the biblical account of Rahab, the Canaanite prostitute who was granted salvation from God because of her courage to hide the two Israelite spies. I thought Amal was comparing me to a "Hollywood woman," whom Muslims consider immoral. I certainly did not want her to think that.

"No, Amal, I am definitely not a prostitute," I replied emphatically. She looked more confused, for she did not understand my word, *prostitute*. She located her Arabic/English dictionary and fingered through the pages until she came to the Religious Vocabulary section.

"You priest?" she asked.

"No, Amal, I am not a priest."

Persistently she pressed once again, "You saint?"

Amused, I replied, "No, Amal, I am not a saint." I wondered what in her mind qualified a person to be a saint. *If only she knew,* I thought, *that I am a sinful, selfish, rebellious woman whose entire guilt and shame have been removed by Jesus Christ.*

Finally Amal came to the word she was seeking. "You nun?" she asked, pronouncing the word more like "noon."

I could not move forward with a friendship with Amal until she could put me neatly in a box.

I concluded that the only way to clarify her confusion and satisfy her curiosity was to answer her. I could not move forward with a friendship with Amal until she could put me neatly in a box. "No, Amal, I am not a nun. But I am like a nun except I am a married nun." *Well,* I thought, *how else can I explain I am a woman dedicated to God for His service in this world?*

At last Amal was satisfied. She had thought so all along. I later discovered that in Arabic the word *rahabah* is the word for "nun." All I had heard her say was "rahab." Once Amal knew how to classify me, our friendship took off nicely.

The Need to Know

It became evident to me years ago that if I am not understood clearly enough by some Muslim women, then before long suspicions will arise and rumors will spread extensively among the different communities. This can effectively create fear and cut off relationships.

When a Christian is unconditionally kind to Muslims, she can at times be viewed with suspicion. A Muslim woman will wonder why a Christian woman desires to have a friendship with her in the first place. What does she want? Why is she being kind? The Muslim may even go so far as to suspect that the Christian is a spy, perhaps with the CIA or the FBI! While unconditional kindness and love is part of who we Christians are because of our heritage in Jesus, it is not easily understood by Muslims. Kindness without an agenda shown to someone outside of one's faith group is confusing for them. If, however, the kindness, hospitality or gift is simply a part of one's profession, then it is understood and even expected because this would be part of their culture, too. They need, therefore, to understand clearly who we are in order to alleviate misunderstanding and confusion.

Furthermore, once a friendship begins to develop, the Muslim woman may face many questions from her community. If the community perceives that a Christian woman is comfortable with a Muslim, is showing her unconditional kindness or is relatively knowledgeable about Islam, alarm bells will sound. The community may tell the Muslim woman she can be friends with a Christian but is not allowed to love her. The greater the Christian's understanding of the Muslim culture, the greater the Muslim need to find a box in which to put that Christian.

We should be prepared, then, for Muslims to ask blunt questions. It is all part of the process of becoming at home with them.

In the same way, we Christians also may question or be suspicious of Muslim women. We, too, may try to put them in a box or profile them. If we hear, for example, zealous, defensive talk about Islam or if we see women covered with face veils, we may conclude that they might threaten our homeland security. Sometimes simply the Muslim's tone of voice frightens the Christian. We have entered an era when both sides are prone to suspicion and distrust.

Who Are You?

Not all Christians, however, are suspicious and distrustful of Muslims. Likewise, not all Muslim women jump to suspicious conclusions. My friend Zahra was not suspicious. She, like hundreds of others, was simply curious to know who I was.

Zahra is a Persian beauty, full of enthusiasm for life. She is smart and chic and a good mother to her children. I mentioned to her that I would be speaking at a Christian women's retreat on the subject of removing the masks we sometimes wear. I told her about the masquerade we were planning. All the attendees were to come to the meeting wearing a mask of their choosing. I planned to wear my wedding veil. The subject intrigued her.

"Who are you?" she asked rather bluntly.

"You know, Zahra," I began to explain, "when we wear a mask we are hiding something. We do not want people to know who we are."

"I do not think I know who I am," Zahra exclaimed. "Do you know who you are?"

"Yes, I do," I replied.

"Who are you?" she asked rather bluntly.

What should I say? I pondered. I thought of the religious leaders who sent priests to John the Baptist in the wilderness to find out his exact identity. The priests asked him bluntly, "Then who are you? We need an answer for those who sent us. What do you have to say about yourself?" (John 1:22). I also thought of the encounter Jesus had with his disciples when He asked, "Who do people say that I am?" They replied that some people thought He was John the Baptist, others said Elijah and still others said He was one of the ancient prophets risen from the dead. Then Jesus asked, "Who do you say I am?" Peter replied that He was the Messiah sent from God. I wanted to be like Peter, who clearly recognized and boldly acknowledged Jesus' kingship in His life.

"Well," I fumbled, groping for a simple way to describe who I am. "I am a little girl inside who knows she is loved by her husband and by God. And actually I love myself."

"Oh," she said, surprised.

"Yes, I like my personality."

Zahra responded, "I like it, too." The conversation was going okay, so I ventured on.

"Actually, Zahra, God is my King and I am His princess."

"Oh, I like that," she said, "but what about Ed, if God is your King?"

"Ed is not my king, Zahra. God is. Ed comes under God. Ed is not God."

"Oh!" She looked confused. And no wonder! Zahra helped me to understand that to say in Persian that I am God's princess implies that I am His wife! I, on the other hand, had meant the phrase to connote a dear, cherished daughter. I am always learning how to communicate more clearly with my Muslim friends, and I am always learning how to jump the cultural and linguistic hurdles between us. The fact that they bear my blunders endears them to me.

Zahra then said, "I do not like what I see in myself. It is bad. I am really selfish." Zahra was removing a mask and inviting me to look. In an honor/shame-based culture, as are the majority of Islamic cultures, it is important to appear good before others. Zahra's honesty was refreshing to me.

For the next hour we discussed the masks we wear and why we wear them. And we talked about having two faces—a public one and a private one. We may be able to fool people by the masks we wear, I told Zahra, but God sees us as we are. Even though we try to hide our faults, He loves us in spite of them.

Horoscopes and Names

When I met Mojgan, the first thing she asked me was what my horoscope sign is. I did not know, which surprised her, so she proceeded to ask my birthday month. When I told her, she stated happily, "Then you are a cat, and I am a dog! We will get along fine." She added, "I have had some bad experiences because some people and I have not been lined up right, and I just wanted to see if everything would be okay between us."

I was rather taken aback at being analyzed in such a strange way, though it appeared Mojgan was accustomed to asking that information immediately upon being introduced to a person. Yet she did not stop there. She proceeded to inquire exactly the day and year I was born. By that time it was clear to me that Mojgan had a big problem with trust and depended on horoscope signs and numerology to know whether or not she would be safe with a new person. I was out of my comfort zone and not sure what to say.

I ventured, "Mojgan, my birthday is completely safe because God planned it, day, year and all." She did not press further. I breathed a prayer of relief.

It is surprising that some Muslim women engage in horoscopes and numerology, since these things are forbidden in Islam. Nevertheless, in many Muslim homes people look to the occult arts to guide them. Hiding their activities from the public, as Zarina and her friends did when they were reading palms in her bedroom, some Muslim women use the occult arts to help them pursue safe relationships, blessings and some measure of control over their lives. Since Allah is impersonal and too great for them to comprehend, they use such aids to try to connect with him and find answers to their questions. They also use occult arts to connect with and answer questions about other people, as Mojgan did with me.

For the Muslim woman, a significant way to determine who a person is can be found in the meaning of the person's name. Muslim names are given because the parents want their child to embody a certain quality or destiny. Names are personal to Muslims, and when we understand what is important to them, they feel more at home with us and we with them.

Hussein stayed in our home for a short while and told me about his sister, Fawziah, who lived in his country. I wrote Fawziah a letter, starting a sort of pen-pal relationship, and asked her what was happening in her life. She wrote back a four-page letter containing the names of her brothers and sisters, what each name meant and how they were fulfilling the destinies of their particular names. The entire letter revolved around the meanings of their names!

Often on first visits with a Muslim woman, I will discuss the meaning of her name, which delights her considerably. Then I will share what my name means.

"*J* is for 'Jesus first,' *O* for 'others second,' and *Y* for 'yourself last.' When I live life in that order, I have *JOY*," I have relayed countless times. They inevitably like my explanation of my name.

Personal Questions

A Muslim woman's questions for us may become even more personal and take on a bluntness with which we might not feel comfortable. Her questions may invade our Western sense of privacy.

"Do you drink alcohol?" "How about your husband or son?" "Do you go swimming?" (When she asks this, I know she is asking if I wear a swimsuit in public, exposing my body to the eyes of men.) "Are you going to have more children?" "Are you a Muslim?" "Do you fast?"

On one initial visit with a Muslim woman, she made it clear that drinking, smoking, public swimming, singing and whistling are completely forbidden. It was as if she was saying that those five things defined who she was. She wanted me to know right from the start that she was a religious woman because she abstained from those activities. As she struggled to figure me out, I also was trying to understand who she was and what made her view life the way she did. I inquired if she thought Allah would punish her for whistling, and she nodded her head emphatically.

"Are you afraid you might go to hell if a man should hear you whistle?" I gently asked her.

"Oh, yes!" she replied. I felt incredibly sorry for this woman. When I got in my car to drive home, I broke out whistling the song "Blessed Assurance," gratefully enjoying my freedom in Christ.

The Muslim woman's husband is also concerned about who we are. Religious Muslim men do not want just any woman to come into their wives' lives, possibly corrupting them with Western values. On the first visit with a Muslim woman, her husband is often present. Besides being polite and hospitable, he is also sizing me up, wanting to know if I am a moral, religious person. He usually gives me the distinct impression that I have to pass some kind of test. He can shut down any further opportunity for me to meet with his wife if he has doubts about me. He is the authority in the family, and it is important to respect that authority and not do anything behind his back, such as taking her shopping, to a park or to church. It is important that the husband know who I am and that I am a safe person.

On my first visit to one Saudi family, the husband immediately wanted me to know that he was not a terrorist. He explained his perception that most Westerners paint Arabs, especially Saudis, as terrorists. It bothered me to see the pain etched on his face from this perceived generalization, and I reassured him that I did not feel that way. We talked about generalizations, and I asked him in return not to think of me as a "Hollywood woman." Suddenly relaxing in his chair, the husband laughed, recognizing how both Muslims and Christians can have distorted perceptions that are exacerbated by the media.

In order for a relationship to move forward with a Muslim woman or family, they need to understand exactly who we are, and personal questions are part of gaining this understanding.

I had passed the test with this Muslim man. He had determined that I was a religious, safe woman, and I was welcomed into his new bride's life—and into their home.

In our culture, marital status, how many children a person has, the meaning of one's name, religious affiliation and practices or moral stances on issues are not usually as important as knowing what a person does. Yet for Muslims these questions are uppermost. In order for a relationship to move forward with a Muslim woman or family, they need to understand exactly who we are, and personal questions are part of gaining this understanding.

6

Virginity

Javed had returned to his country during the summer holidays to marry. Now he had returned to Canada to complete his graduate studies, bringing with him his bride of one month. He was concerned that Nabila, so new to our country, was uncomfortable being left alone in the apartment while he did his research at the university. She followed him to the campus and waited around there but was bored. The days were long, and she was not used to being alone. In her country she had always been surrounded by family or friends. Javed wanted me to meet Nabila and help make her adjustment to staying at home easier. I had passed his test, and now he trusted me.

Nabila was shy and submissive, but vivacious and attractive. Being a brand-new wife, she was all dolled up. You would have thought she was about to go to a party with her fingernails manicured and polished, her makeup perfectly applied and her gold wedding jewelry dripping off her. As I sat with her in their apartment looking over her beautiful wedding photos, I asked, "Nabila, how did you and Javed meet?"

"A cousin of mine knew Javed and his family," she replied, "and then he told my parents about him. They checked out Javed and his family. He comes from a good family. His dad is a doctor. My family and Javed's family talked it over and arranged our marriage. But before the arrangement was accepted we wanted to meet each other. So one day Javed, along with his parents, requested to meet me in my parents' home. I was nervous to meet him. He had one hundred requirements for me to meet. It was like an examination. He studied everything, even how I walked or cast my eyes. He had really high requirements. Other girls had not passed his examination. But I did!" Nabila obviously was proud of this achievement.

"Oh, my goodness! A hundred requirements? A wife would have to be perfect. What were Javed's highest requirements for a wife?" I asked incredulously.

"She had to be educated, religious and beautiful."

"What do you mean by religious?" I queried.

She thought for a moment. "She has to wear the *hijab*."

Yes, I had learned over the years that wearing a *hijab* is a strong statement. The woman who wears the *hijab* believes she is pleasing Allah because he has commanded her in the Qur'an to wear it. She strives to be an obedient, modest woman, and the *hijab* unmistakably identifies her as a Muslim. *Hijabs* come in a bright array of colors and are often made of silk or chiffon. Some are even adorned with beads, ribbon or embroidery, and they are worn in various attractive ways. Most Muslim women are convinced that wearing the *hijab* protects them from inappropriate sexual advances from men. Many have reminded me that Mary (Maryam), the mother of Jesus, wore a *hijab*. After all, we would not recognize Mary without her head covered, would we? Furthermore, they point out, nuns have worn head coverings since long before the *hijab* came on the scene. So, they ask, why don't all Christian women wear them?

Without waiting for an answer, she asked bluntly, "Was he your boyfriend?"

"Hmm," I responded. "That makes a woman religious?"

"Yes," Nabila said, as if that should be clear. "She pleases Allah when she wears the *hijab*." Then she inquired, "How did you meet your husband, Joy?" Nabila had heard about Western women having boyfriends and sleeping with them out of wedlock. Without waiting for an answer, she asked bluntly, "Was he your boyfriend?" I knew Nabila was really asking if I had been a virgin when I married. To her, the word *boyfriend* implied sleeping with a man before marriage. I did not feel comfortable with Nabila's question. It would take some time to get used to my privacy being invaded.

A Matter of Morals and Honor

Virginity is a moral value upheld by Muslims worldwide. A young woman's virginity is of utmost importance to Muslims because it is a matter of honor or shame for her family. Her virginity is not simply an individual matter, as it is in the West. If a Muslim woman has had sexual relations before marriage, then she brings shame upon her entire family. Yet if she is a virgin when she marries, it is a badge of honor. This is why Muslims monitor their daughters' public freedom and train their daughters from an early age to dress modestly. Muslim families want to protect their daughters from the sexual freedom of our culture and fear their daughters may follow the ways of "Christians," meaning Westerners. Some girls may start wearing the *hijab* as young as five years old, although I have seen one as young as two wearing it! They are conditioned to accept modesty from an early age, and this modesty is tightly linked with staying sexually pure before marriage. Occasionally when a young girl wears a *hijab* it signifies that she is pledged to be married to a certain man when she gets older.

This is a major difference between our two cultures. Our Western worldview holds the individual responsible for his or her actions. If a girl wants to sleep with her boyfriend, that is her business. But Muslims have a shame/honor worldview that maintains a collective sense of responsibility. It took years for me to understand the honor/shame worldview of Islamic nations. For them, shame is a painful affliction. They strive for the family's name to be honored.

If a woman is a virgin when she marries, it is a badge of honor.

Moral purity of women is not only an individual or family ideal, but it is also a national one. In 2006 a "Miss Muslim" contest was held in Tatarstan, much like Miss America. Yet unlike Miss America, the competitors could not wear swimsuits; they had to be modestly dressed and wear *hijabs*. The goal of the pageant was to show that beauty does not have anything to do with nudity or immodesty. It was a contest to reveal intelligence and religiosity. The contest included memorization and recitation of the Qur'an, as well as cooking and sewing. Contestants were graded based upon how they brought honor to their families, countries, religion and Allah. A young virgin from Tatarstan won the contest. As this contest proved, beauty, purity and morality are family and national values in Muslim countries.

A Contract versus a Covenant

Realizing where Nabila was coming from when she asked if Ed was my boyfriend, I replied, "Yes, Ed was my boyfriend for four years, but we did not sleep together. I was a virgin when I married. We did many fun things together, such as going out to eat and taking walks together. Two years of that time Ed was in Canada and I was in Chicago."

Nabila could not believe I was truly a virgin when I married. "Ed was a virgin, too, Nabila," I added. Shock and amazement registered on her face.

"Is everyone in your country a virgin when they marry—both men and women?" I probed.

"Well," she replied, shifting her position on the couch, "if a girl is not a virgin, it can be proved. But for the man it is not such a big problem."

"Nabila, did you know that in the Bible it is written that God's plan is for sex to be reserved for marriage?"

"Our Qur'an says that, too," she affirmed, but she was surprised that the Bible said the same thing.

"A lot of people aren't virgins, though. Did you know God can forgive them? A person's life is not over because they have sinned." I began to expound on the forgiving character of God. For Nabila, however, losing one's virginity was the ultimate offense for a woman.

"We do not have boyfriends and girlfriends in my country," Nabila stated matter-of-factly. "It is important that we are virgins when we marry. Things are changing nowadays, and some people date, but most do not approve of that. Our parents usually arrange our marriages."

"Can you refuse to marry the person they arrange for you to marry?" I asked.

"Yes, but usually they know best. If anything goes wrong, then the parents are responsible to deal with it. Joy, what were Ed's requirements for a wife?"

"Well, his wife had to be a Christian," I replied. "But I am not sure what other requirements he was looking for. I know that for me it was really important that my husband be a kind man. His looks, education or wealth were not as significant to me as his character. He just had to be kind. And he is."

"You are really lucky," Nabila said slowly, her voice trailing off quietly. I could tell she was worried about something but could not voice it.

She got up and went into her bedroom, bringing back with her the marriage contract she and Javed had signed. I was shocked. It looked more like a contract for divorce than marriage! It was pages and pages long, and it outlined many expectations and conditions, including conditions upon which divorce could be legitimized. If there were no children, for instance, Javed would be allowed to take another wife. I was reminded of my friend Laleh, who had not conceived a child after fifteen years of marriage. Her husband told her that if she did not get pregnant after one last medical procedure, then he would marry another woman, whom his father had already selected. I began to see that while virginity is a qualification for marriage, Muslims have many other conditions and requirements after marriage that can cause a woman to fear losing her sense of unconditional acceptance.

It was the first time Nabila had heard about a covenant relationship.

I shared with Nabila about the wedding vows Ed and I made. I told her that we had promised to be faithful to each other until death separated us and that our marriage was not a contract but a covenant. It was not based upon my health or beauty, or whether I could produce children, or any other condition. It was the first time Nabila had heard about a covenant relationship.

We spent the rest of our time together that day flipping through Nabila's photo album. It was obvious that a lot of money had been spent on Javed and Nabila's wedding. As she answered my many questions, I learned a great deal about Muslim wedding customs and traditions.

I dropped by often after that initial visit, finding Nabila easy to love.

Shame versus Grace

Nabila and I spent many other visits together talking about the gifts of forgiveness, grace and mercy that are abundantly provided by Jesus Christ. I tried to help her understand that we all are guilty of breaking God's moral laws, including whether or not we are virgins at the time of marriage. I wanted her to know that no offense is too great for God to forgive, to grasp the absolute purity of God's holiness and to understand the meaning not only of outward purity but also of inner purity. And I wanted Nabila to see that Jesus is able to remove our shame through His atoning sacrifice on the cross. He can lift us to the honorable position of being a saint in His eyes—not because of our goodness or moral purity, but because He removes our guilt and shame.

How I longed to help Nabila understand more about Christianity! I prayed she would learn that life is not about appearing pure, but rather, it is about a relationship with Jesus Christ, who makes us pure with His righteousness.

It often takes a long time for Muslims to understand and accept by faith these wonderful truths found in Christ. But the process of exploring each other's beliefs and differing worldviews helped us to feel at home with each other.

We talked in the context of mutual respect and friendship, rather than merely gleaning information from books or the media.

Nevertheless, I could see that there were obvious, vast differences between our two faiths.

7

A New Kind of Praying

Muslims and Christians both believe in praying, but our praying is quite different. Karima taught me that.

Karima is one of the most delightful, enjoyable, loving Muslim women I have met. She and Abdul had recently arrived in Canada when I met them. Abdul had inquired at the university's International Center about someone who could help his wife with English. The center contacted me, and I consented to help.

Abdul and Karima lived far from my home, and parking was difficult where they lived, so once a week I took the bus and then walked a distance to visit her. I knew this would require commitment during the cold winter months. Furthermore, I had to leave my comfort zone, as their apartment was not in a safe area, and rough, drunk men often surrounded me on their elevator.

But it did not take long for me to become attached to this family. They were kindhearted and laughed a lot. Abdul and Karima had both taught at the same university in their country, where they fell in love and married. It was delightful to observe their respectful, loving relationship. Abdul was considerate and genuinely kind to Karima.

Having an avid interest in cultures, I asked Abdul and Karima many questions about theirs. My obvious interest in their land made them feel comfortable. They had noticed that few North Americans were aware of the famous history of their country, so my asking questions endeared me to them. Both are quite bright and wanted to pursue graduate studies in the West. After they arrived in Canada, however, only Abdul pursued studies since baby Jamal came into their lives.

As I spent time with Karima week after week, I learned a great deal about her and her religion. I learned that her understanding of praying was reciting prescribed prayers at five specified times of the day. While she sometimes whispered requests extemporaneously, she considered those prayers to be less valuable than the ones prescribed.

The Call to Prayer

One day as we were studying English, I was stunned to hear a cleric from across the ocean calling Karima to prayer through her computer! "Oh, my goodness, Karima! What was that?" I asked incredulously. I was pretty sure it was the call to prayer, but here in my country? I noticed that the clock and a prayer schedule posted on her refrigerator also indicated it was time to say prayers.

> *I was stunned to hear a cleric from across the ocean calling Karima to prayer through her computer!*

"Oh, that is the prayer call from my city. Excuse me, Joy, I need to pray. It will take only a few minutes." Interrupting our English lesson and leaving me in her living room, Karima quickly got up and went to her bathroom, where she performed some ablutions to make her body physically and ceremonially clean before Allah, for this was mandatory.

I had learned of this requirement before. When my friend Ruma bought gifts for her family back in Bangladesh, I asked her what she was planning to give them.

"Artificial fingernails," she answered.

Surprised and not understanding why artificial nails would be so desirable, I asked, "Why?"

She replied, "We should not wear fingernail polish or makeup when we say our prayers. Allah would not be pleased. It is easier and more convenient simply to remove artificial nails than to remove fingernail polish."

After Karima completed her ablutions and donned her white prayer clothes, which are used only for praying, she came out and spread her prayer carpet close beside me, ensuring that the attached compass was pointing east toward Mecca, the direction Muslims believe Allah has instructed them to face. She then began the prayer ritual of various motions: kneeling, rising, turning her head right and left. At one point she turned to me while quietly muttering the words and smiled at me. I smiled back. When she was finished, she quickly returned to our English lesson. The ritual had been completed.

How Do I Pray?

I soon discovered that Karima was grieving the loss of her father, who had died a few months before she had moved to Canada. She was visibly distressed about her widowed mother back home and needed comfort. Seeing her sadness and grief, I greatly desired to pray for her, but I wondered how to go about it. I knew she had never attended a church service or a Christian prayer meeting to observe how Christians pray out loud for each other and about any concern on our hearts. I knew our conversational method of prayer would be quite different for her. It is more of a dialogue with God, rather than a monologue, and its tone is often one of casual friendship. Rather than kneeling, we Christians usually just pray where we are, and we do not cover our heads. We also do not prepare ourselves first with ablutions. And we do not face a certain direction, for our Father is present everywhere and within us.

I debated how to introduce my desire to pray for her. Would she be offended? The Christian faith is difficult to introduce because it is foreign and unfamiliar to Muslims. Rather than a master/slave relationship to which they are accustomed, our faith is centered on a father/child relationship. I decided it was too cumbersome to go into all the differences, so I just forged ahead.

"Karima, may I pray for you?" I asked. "You know, God really does care about your grief, and He can comfort you. When I pray, I speak to God in heaven in the name of Jesus. Would you like me to pray for you?"

Not knowing what it meant to have someone pray for her right then, she just nodded her head, appreciating that I cared for her. "I mean right here with you now," I explained further.

"Okay," she agreed. This was new to her. We both raised our hands, palms opened toward God, a posture that was familiar to her.

I prayed, "Dear God in heaven, I speak to You in the name of Jesus Christ, my wonderful Savior and Comforter. My friend Karima is really hurting because her dad died, and she is worried about her mother. Would You please comfort her? Help her to understand who Jesus is and that He understands our pain and grief. In the name of Jesus, amen." It was short, simple and childlike.

Tears running down her face, Karima sat there quietly for a few minutes. I let her be touched by the presence of the Holy Spirit. He was ministering to her, and I did not want to ruin the sacred moment. I, too, was enveloped with a sense of awe and beauty.

Karima looked up at me and said almost in a whisper, "No one has ever prayed for me before."

After a while, Karima looked up at me and said almost in a whisper, "No one has ever prayed for me before." Choked with emotion, I breathed silently, *Oh God, what a blessed privilege to pray for Muslim women like Karima!*

She was filled with wonderment at this new kind of praying. I imagine Jesus' disciples must have experienced the same sense after they asked Him to teach them how to pray and then heard Him demonstrate an altogether new kind of praying. Jesus, whose praying went beyond rituals, actually taught them a lot of truths while He prayed.

Praying for Muslims

Muslims have a respect for prayer. I have prayed with hundreds of Muslim women of all kinds: educated, uneducated, village people, city people, rich, poor, fundamentalists, secularized Muslims, mystic Sufis, those steeped in folk Islam and even a woman who actually called herself a terrorist. Out of all of them, I recall only one woman who declined my offer to pray. She begged me to pray for her before her surgery, but after the successful surgery she did not want prayer. Other than that, not one single Muslim woman has disturbed or halted my praying, although one fundamentalist woman got up and walked around while I was praying and then asked curtly, "Are you finished?" Numerous times Muslim women have interrupted my prayer to ask me to ask God for something—help with an upcoming exam or a mother's health, for example. Occasionally a Muslim will interject an "Ameen" (Amen) throughout my prayers. Often Muslims join me in saying "Ameen" at the end of my praying, surprised that we say the same word.

After praying, their response is usually much like Karima's. They stare a bit in shock, dazed and mystified. Some begin to cry, while others sit misty-eyed and mumble a sincere thank-you.

Praying in the name of Jesus touches Muslims deeply in their souls.

Praying in the name of Jesus touches Muslims deeply in their souls. I believe the Spirit of Jesus comes into our midst and is active, touching them and revealing Himself to them. I speak with God, not to the Muslim, when I pray. I am demonstrating a new kind of relationship with God, unknown to them. I have found that demonstrating this new kind of praying in a father/child relationship is often much easier than explaining it to my Muslim friends.

A Foundation of Trust and Love

The more I prayed for Karima, the stronger the foundation of trust and love became. She introduced me to her North African friends, with whom I began meeting weekly, too. They all came to the wedding of one of our children. It was their first time to enter a church building and to witness a Christian wedding.

"Joy, the hair on my arms stood up during the wedding. It was so different. I cannot explain what I felt," Karima joyously relayed. It was a sacred and powerful occasion, and I knew she had been affected by the simplicity, beauty and holiness of a Christian wedding.

It was obvious Karima was a sincere, practicing Muslim. She loved her faith, and she did not find Islam burdensome, much to my surprise. She was faithful in wearing her head covering, never answering a knock at her door without first covering her head. From her apartment, which overlooked a park, she often watched people and was horrified to see Westerners kissing and lying together on the grass or bikini-clad women tanning. She felt safe in her apartment away from them. She was concerned that three-year-old Jamal would be contaminated and influenced by this moral corruption. I tried to stress to her, as I do to all my Muslim friends, that my marriage with my husband operates in love, friendship, trust and respect. Abdul and Karima watched us closely and were irresistibly attracted to our marriage. They were surprised to discover we had been married for over thirty years.

Karima miscarried shortly after arriving in Canada and found this difficult to handle. Far from the comfort of her mother, she was lonely and in pain. I gave her a card to express my comfort and hugged her tenderly. At that moment I did not see her as a Muslim or myself as a Christian. We were simply women who understood the things that touch womanhood. That card spoke volumes to her. She treasured it.

I had many opportunities to pray for Karima, and she always welcomed it. It was not long before Karima became pregnant again, and this time she gave birth to a beautiful baby girl. When we got the call, we immediately dropped everything and went to the hospital. Over the next months we enjoyed cuddling that irresistibly adorable Arab baby with her typically full head of black hair.

Shortly after the birth, Karima began to experience abdominal pain and had to undergo surgery. We took Karima and Abdul to the hospital. She was frightened, especially when the orderly approached to wheel her away to the operating room.

"Oh, Joy, please pray for me," she begged, trembling with apprehension. She calmed immediately after I prayed. Abdul, who loved his wife dearly and was deeply concerned for her at that moment, was touched and shook his head in disbelief, saying, "None of our people would do this for us. They offer help but never carry through with it." Indeed, every community fails and disappoints its members at some point.

Readiness

Over the years I prayed many times for Karima. I prayed prayers of blessing after the baby was born. I prayed for Abdul's stress level in his graduate studies. When it was time for Karima to leave Canada, I prayed a farewell benediction over her and her family. And when we bid farewell in front of all her Arab Muslim friends she unashamedly hugged me. "I love you, Karima," I whispered in her ear as I hugged her. She held me tight and started crying and replied, "I love you, too, Joy." When I got home I let my tears flow freely. I have had to say such difficult goodbyes many times, and each time I wish love did not have to bring pain.

I was always more than ready to share Jesus with Karima, but she was not ready to hear much. She remained afraid to ask questions about my faith, right to the end of our time together. Entertaining questions is not encouraged in her faith. Every time I brought up the subject, Karima would direct the conversation to a safer topic. She never was ready to accept a Bible. Like most Muslims, Karima considered Islam to be the best religion and Mohammed the last prophet, so she saw no need to ask questions anyway. Karima always gave the impression that she was afraid to find out about Christianity.

How I yearned for our spirits to be united as sisters in Jesus! I did not want only to pray for Karima, but that was as far as she allowed me to go. I begged God many times to draw Karima to Jesus. I cried for her, because I loved her deeply. I wanted—no, I yearned desperately with all my being for us to be sisters in Jesus. I knew that only the Holy Spirit could open Karima's eyes and make her ready to see and hear His truths.

But one thing was certain: Karima was always ready for me to pray for her. And I know that my prayers through Jesus Christ taught her a great deal. Sometimes we Christians have to be read like a letter for a long time before others are ready to hear the truth.

8

Afraid to Know

As I visited a church one Sunday, I began chatting with a well-dressed woman in the lobby. I could not figure out where she came from. I started telling her about having lived in Muslim lands, and then in a hushed voice Sue, as she preferred to be called, disclosed that she was a Muslim Uighur from China's most western province. I was surprised to meet her in a church, knowing that she came from an ethnic group that has had little opportunity to hear the full story of Jesus Christ.

Thousands of Muslims like Sue live in North America. Living in this Land of Many Churches does not necessarily mean that she has clearly heard the Gospel. Christianity is as unfamiliar to Muslims as Islam is to us, and Muslim women like Sue usually have misconceptions about Christianity that will need to be corrected with a gentle and wise spirit.

As a follower of Islam, the Muslim woman will speak passionately about her holy book, the Qur'an, and profess a zealous belief in her *nabi* ("prophet"), Mohammed. She respects

Jesus Christ, believing Him to be an important prophet who performed miracles and healings. She acknowledges that Jesus was born of the virgin Mary and will return to the world a second time. But she will not agree that He is the Son of God or God incarnate. She does not believe she needs a Savior to forgive her sins. According to the Qur'an, Jesus did not die on the cross, was not buried and did not rise from the dead. The mysteries of the Christian faith will take a long time for her to understand and accept by faith. Even though it is challenging to talk about the cross and difficult for the Muslim to understand, the cross must remain central to our Gospel presentation. Furthermore, she will say that she believes in the Bible but that it has been changed and superseded by the Qur'an. A common misconception is that Christians believe in three gods: Creator, Jesus and Mary.

Yet in attempting to give Muslims the Gospel message, we often encounter great fear. It is this fear that often separates us, and it is this fear that keeps them from asking questions.

Fear Grips Sue

I learned that Sue had visited the church a few times during her one-year stay and was to return to China in a month. I asked if she had been given a Bible or *Injil* ("the gospels"), if the story of Jesus Christ had been explained to her or if she had seen a movie about Him. She had not received any information. She had been eager to hear the story of the Bible explained to her, but everyone in the church had seemed too busy.

We arranged a time to meet the following week. I found a movie about Jesus Christ in the Uighur language for her. But just before our scheduled meeting Sue called, and I could tell fear had gripped her. We could not meet. This time it was she who was too busy.

No one knew she was an Uighur Muslim. Sue had disclosed that private knowledge only to me. The possibility of that sensitive information being discovered made her fearful, as it could potentially jeopardize her future career with the Chinese government. After all, an Uighur Muslim, a minority in China, often does not get many opportunities for advancement. She did not want any potentially dangerous rumors to follow her back to China.

I asked if I could leave a package of the Bible and video at the church for her to pick up, but she declined and said she wanted no more contact with me. I was greatly disappointed, but I knew she would be here three more weeks and waited to see if she would change her mind. I respected her request for no contact. I did not have her phone number, address or even her last name, making contact impossible anyway.

A Spiritual Battle

Often when I have shared the Good News of Jesus Christ with a Muslim woman, I have come up against fear, confusion, misunderstanding, opposition, suspicion, resistance, caution and disinterest. My natural reaction is to feel shaky and weak, and my timid nature begins to surface. I have learned to identify these as telltale signs of a spiritual battle, and they sometimes make me want to run away from friendships with Muslim women. I did not feel strong enough for this kind of challenge with Sue, nor did I feel at home in the midst of this spiritual battle. I knew I needed prayer support and immediately notified our Emergency Prayer Community (EPC).

After settling back into life in North America and knowing God wanted us to share the Good News of Christ with Muslims here, Ed and I formed this group to support us in prayer. Its members hail from California to Nunavut and are Americans, Canadians, Christian Arabs, Filipinos and Chinese. They represent individuals from many denominations—Baptist, Presbyterian, Pentecostal, Anglican, Mennonite, Christian and Missionary Alliance, nondenominational and charismatic. The spiritual harvest and goal of making Jesus known to the nations unites us. They stand with us in prayer, lift our weary spirits when the going gets tough, offer us timely counsel and open their homes to us when necessary. When we cry for help, they listen and pray. They pour out hidden sacrificial prayer, day and night, on our behalf and are invaluable to us and our ministry. Our EPC is spiritually robust and understands the nature of spiritual battles, even as they stand behind the scenes of frontline activity.

One day Sue phoned me and was obviously distressed. "Please stop calling me and leaving messages on my phone."

"I haven't called you at all, Sue," I replied. She seemed confused and surprised. I discerned quickly that Satan's opposing forces were working to prevent her from hearing the Good News of Jesus Christ.

My heart ached for this bright, young woman who was torn with desire to know but controlled and prevented by fear.

She added, "And please stop posting your messages on my door."

"Sue, I haven't been posting any messages," I assured her. She hung up without further conversation. That was the last I ever talked with her. She flew back to China. My heart ached for this bright, young woman who was torn with the desire to know but was controlled and prevented by fear.

Fear at Work

Whereas secular Westerners usually avoid conversations about religious matters and disagreements, generally speaking Muslims enjoy talking about such topics. This is one of the things I love about them. I am most at home with people who love to talk about God. But when I observe fear at work my heart becomes sad. Satan fears the truth of the Gospel, and he does not want Muslims to hear it. He tries hard to prevent or hinder a hearing.

After finishing supper in our home, Mazin from Saudi Arabia wanted to peruse the Arabic Bible he saw on our living room bookshelf. The words of life captured his attention as he read them for the first time. Before he left our house, we asked if we could take his photo. Suddenly he noticed that the Bible was on the couch beside him, and he quickly moved to cover it with a cushion. If it is a holy book, as Muslims consider it to be, why did Mazin feel compelled to hide it? One word: *fear*.

I saw fear at work in Areej, too. She was a young mother from the eastern part of Africa whose husband was nearing the completion of his graduate studies. Like Sue, Areej had a pressing question but was afraid to ask. Unable to keep quiet any longer, she finally mustered her courage to ask me about the perplexing issue on her mind.

> ***Satan fears the truth of the Gospel, and he does not want Muslims to hear it.***

"Oh, Joy, before you leave I have a question. My husband's friend just finished his Ph.D., and he had a flight booked to return to our country when he took his own life. Does your Book say anything about where he would go?"

Catching my breath at the shocking news, I replied, "Oh, Areej, I am so sorry to hear that dreadful news. The Bible does not speak specifically about committing suicide, though it does tell stories of people who did. But one thing I know is that your husband's friend must have had some deep pain that he could not bear. And I know that God loved him and understood his pain and would have been sad that he had not discovered how much God loved him."

"Could you get me a Bible, Joy?" she asked, wanting to check it out. It had taken great courage for her to request a Bible. *Yes, Lord!* I inwardly shouted.

A week later I returned to Areej with an Arabic Bible. Standing in the middle of the living room, she opened it randomly to 1 Timothy 3:2 and began reading out loud, "Now the overseer must be above reproach, the husband of but one wife, temperate, self-controlled, respectable, hospitable, able to teach" (NIV). Closing the Bible, she exclaimed, "I must show this to all my friends in this building!" For a husband to be told in a holy book to have only one wife was attention-grabbing news to her, since her book said a man could have four wives. I wondered where this would lead. It hit a raw nerve in Areej, as it does with many Muslim women, especially those who are threatened with the prospect of sharing their husbands with another wife. Some of the women defend the passage in the Qur'an permitting a man to have more than one wife by informing me that their men do not have girlfriends or affairs, like "Christian" married men do. At least their men legally marry, they argue. Others, however, shudder even at the mention of the possibility.

The next week Areej offered me about thirty cassette tapes on Islam, which someone at the mosque had given her. She had not been given permission to ask more questions. It was sad that her fear kept her from knowing about or reading the Bible.

Such fear can even develop into a fear of being around a Christian, particularly one who is clear and knowledgeable about her beliefs. Such was the case of Najla.

We were having a great evening eating and chatting in our home when she posed a question: "Joy, do you know the one—just the one thing—that makes you a Christian?"

"Sure," I replied.

Before I could explain, Najla further elaborated, "Quite a few Christian women in the mosque have become Muslims. I asked them what had made them Christians before, and not one of them could answer my question. Do you know what one thing makes you a Christian?" I got the impression she thought she had stumped me.

Opening my Bible, I read, "If you confess with your mouth that Jesus is Lord and believe in your heart that God raised him from the dead, you will be saved" (Romans 10:10).

"I do not have any problem with that," Najla quickly answered.

"Really?" I asked incredulously. I read the verse again. "You believe that Jesus is Lord, or God?"

"Never!" she replied emphatically, looking aghast.

"How about believing that Jesus died and was raised to life?" I bore down on the exacting truths of the Gospel message.

"No, Jesus did not die, so He was not buried. And He was taken off the cross still alive and was not raised to life." Najla spoke pointedly, as if she was a teacher.

"Well, Najla, you cannot be a Christian until you can confess that Jesus is Lord, did die and was raised from the dead. Just as I cannot become a Muslim until I declare the *shahada*—the declaration that 'there is no god but Allah, and Mohammed is the prophet of Allah.'" After that, Najla became afraid to be around me because I knew what the Word of God said.

Fear separates people.

Fear separates people. When Muslims are bound by fear, it can become nearly impossible for Muslims and Christians to have a relationship with each other. It is for Muslims like these that I especially intercede, asking the Holy Spirit to remove the veil over their eyes so they might glimpse our Savior in all His glory and majesty.

But for the Holy Spirit

While many Muslims remain afraid to read the Bible or ask questions, we still have hope! Praise the Lord that the Holy Spirit can break through this fear in Muslims' lives so that they become delightfully captured with the beauty and purity of the Word of God and convinced of the saving power of Jesus Christ!

The Holy Spirit is moving like a mighty river across the Islamic nations today. The rushing waters cannot be stopped. Literally hundreds of women who have come out of Islam and turned to Jesus are gathering together in large, organized conferences with hearts on fire to worship and grow in their knowledge of Scripture. It truly feels like "Home, Sweet Home" when I sit among groups of Muslim women who have decided to follow Jesus. The Holy Spirit is making waves in these exciting days, and we have the privilege of riding them! It is God's *kairos* time in history, and what a blessed joy to witness it in our lifetime!

9

Christmas and Easter

It was Hawa's first Christmas in the West, and I gave her a stuffed white bear with a bright red ribbon around its neck. She was delighted with it, as it was the first stuffed animal she had received in her 25 years. Forever after she kept it sitting on top of her refrigerator.

Life had thrown Hawa a cruel blow. She had watched both her mother and father gunned down in their house in Somalia. With no time to bury them, in a panic she had fled the house to save her life, taking nothing with her, not even a photo, and had ridden in a truck on a long, bumpy journey to a refugee camp in Kenya.

Now it was my turn to be surprised. Even though Hawa could not afford to buy anything besides her basic daily needs, she handed me a small, wrapped Christmas gift and watched for my response. I opened the gift in disbelief. Little cross earrings? From a Somali Muslim woman?

"Oh, Hawa, thank you so much! The earrings are lovely. Do you know the story about the cross?" I asked.

"No, I do not know any story about the cross. I just saw the earrings in the store and thought you would like them," she answered. She simply knew that the cross belonged to the Christians, and because I am a Christian it would mean something to me.

"I do like them very much. May I share a story about the cross with you, Hawa?"

"Yes," she replied. Holding the delicate cross earrings in my hand, I shared the story of Christmas and Easter with Hawa, who heard it for the first time. Her entire life she had been deprived of the privilege of hearing the Gospel account so familiar to us in the West. Who would have imagined that the Christmas and Easter story would be told using earrings?

Hind

Hind had recently arrived from a war-torn region. "Is this Jesus?" Hind asked, showing me a Christmas card with an Eastern Orthodox–looking depiction of Mary holding baby Jesus. "I think it is supposed to be Jesus, but I do not see any tree in the picture," she added. I looked at the crumpled card and wondered where she got it.

"Yes, this is Jesus," I affirmed.

"When we moved into this apartment a week ago, we found it in the garbage," my Muslim friend explained. "Why would anyone throw a picture of Jesus in the garbage?" Hind was confused, as she considered it dishonorable to treat a prophet of God like that.

> *"Why would anyone throw a picture of Jesus in the garbage?"*

"I will always treasure this," she said softly, as she looked lovingly at the partly ripped and crumpled card. I asked her if she knew more of the story of Jesus.

"Yes, I do," Hind answered. Surprised, I asked her what she knew. Like most Muslims, she knew that the Qur'an states the virgin Mary gave birth to Jesus, but she expected a tree, or cross, to be depicted with Him.

I probed further, "Do you understand who this baby Jesus is?"

"Yes, He is the Son of God." Whoa! I was surprised at her quick and definite response, which was considerably different from the majority of Muslims. They typically understand the term *Son of God* to mean that God had union with Mary and Jesus was born from that union. Of course, such a thought is both untrue and repulsive. But Hind understood correctly, as she had seen movies about Jesus on TV in her country. She was not opposed to the truths of the Bible, but the magnitude of the truths had not sunk in fully. It was a delight going over the story again with her, and I prayed silently that she would understand and accept more truth. She was on the way, moving toward putting her faith in Jesus Christ.

While many Christians look for articulate decisions and to hear the familiar sinner's prayer, my eyes are open to observing the slightest movement toward Christ. We never know exactly at what point one enters the Kingdom of God. I was beginning to feel at home with Hind.

Bushra

While Hawa was ignorant about Christmas and Easter, and Hind had some knowledge but also some confusion, Bushra was completely confused. Our Western culture sent her many mixed messages about the Christian faith.

I first met Bushra at a festival of nations in the local park. She and her husband, Abdullah, were new immigrants to our country. Before immigrating she had enjoyed a high-paying professional job. Abdullah soon began the process of qualifying as an engineer in our country. Today they live in a large, new house in an upscale suburban neighborhood. Bushra is a Muslim, although more of a cultural or secular one, and loves Western ways and freedom. She has been hurt by criticism from her Muslim community for not wearing the *hijab* and for wearing clothes considered too tight and revealing. She does not say prayers or keep the fast, which some in her community condemn. Bushra and Abdullah are a bright, energetic couple who are trying to sort out all the facets and nuances of our multicultural and pluralistic society.

Christmas season was particularly confusing to them initially. The malls aggressively enticed people to buy gifts while playing favorite traditional secular songs such as "I'm Dreaming of a White Christmas" followed by Christian songs such as "Away in a Manger." Then there was Santa Claus, who took boys and girls on his lap promising to give them their Christmas wishes. Streets and homes were beautifully lit up with decorated Christmas trees shining through living room windows. *But what are those reindeer all about?* they wondered. And the Christmas program at the English language school was a strange presentation of Santa and all his elves dressed up as his mistresses. A nativity scene displayed on a store shelf depicted Joseph, Mary, the wise men, shepherds, angels and even baby Jesus as snowmen! In another nativity scene, Joseph, Mary and baby Jesus were portrayed as bears. No wonder Bushra and Abdullah, along with many Muslims, were so confused when they came to our country!

Bushra was captivated by one particular song. She had practiced it many times on her keyboard and, proud of her musical ability, she asked me to come hear her sing it. As I sat in her living room, feeling right at home with her, I listened in amazement to my Muslim friend play and sing "O Holy Night" heartily and unabashedly many times over. It was the first Christmas concert by a Muslim that I had ever attended! She momentarily stopped singing and turned to me. "Joy," she asked, "what does it mean when it says the world lay pining in sin and error?"

The time had come to explain to Bushra the reason for the Christmas story. I asked if I could read to her from the Bible. She agreed. We sat at her kitchen table, her head leaning forward with anticipation as she listened.

It was the first Christmas concert by a Muslim that I had ever attended!

Suddenly sitting back, Bushra interrupted my reading to ask, "But where is the part about Santa Claus?" I explained to my Muslim friend that, contrary to some Muslims' initial understanding, Santa Claus is not Jesus, and he is not found in the Bible. And no, Jesus did not look like Santa Claus when He lived here on earth.

Indeed, our cultural customs and traditions regarding the Christmas season are confusing to the newcomer. Even the biblical story itself, so easily understood and taken for granted by us, can be bewildering to the Muslim because of its unfamiliar truths and concepts.

Mohammed, Fatima and a Candy Cane

I did not want Mohammed and Fatima to be confused between our secular and religious Christmas and Easter. I was privileged to tell them the pure, simple Christmas and Easter account in its fullness for the first time.

We were visiting our Muslim friends to deliver toys to needy refugee children. I tucked some red, white and green striped candy canes in my purse to give to Mohammed and Fatima's children. Taking them out of my purse, I asked the couple if I could share the Christmas story with them. They agreed, and the whole family listened attentively as I used the candy canes to illustrate the combined story of Christmas and Easter. I explained how the white color represented Jesus, the pure and sinless Savior who came into the world on Christmas Day.

"Man did not become God, but rather, God became a human being," I carefully explained, saying each word slowly. I waited to see their reaction. This foundational truth, which is the essence of Christmas, could not be avoided simply because it might be offensive to them. I knew they would not be able to process or accept this truth apart from the Holy Spirit. I saw their eyes flinch, and they became quiet as they tried to absorb what to them was a radical statement.

"In Islam we do not believe that," Mohammed abruptly protested.

"Do you believe God can do anything?" I asked them.

"Yes, we believe God can do anything," Fatima answered.

I did not press that point any further but went on to the next point. "The red stripes on the candy cane represent the blood of Jesus Christ shed on the cross for forgiveness of our sins. His life was given as a sacrifice for our sins." They did not understand what the word *sacrifice* meant or why it was necessary to have a sacrifice to atone for our sins. According to Islam, each person is responsible for his own sins. Nobody else can atone for one's sins. I had to take considerable time, therefore, to explain to them the foreign concept of sacrifice. I then moved on to the third color.

"The green color," I said, "symbolizes life and how Jesus rose from the dead, defeating Satan and the power of death. He gives us eternal life. This is why Jesus left His home in heaven and came to earth at Christmas." Their eyes reflected incredulity but a desire to hear more.

They became more amazed when I explained why the candy cane looked like a shepherd's staff. "Do you know what a shepherd is?" I asked. Mohammed had been a camel herder before coming to our country, so I was pretty certain he would understand what a shepherd was.

"Yes, we have lots of shepherds in our country." They nodded their heads with understanding and sudden interest. I knew they were fond of animals, and any story containing animals grabbed their attention.

"Well, Jesus is called the Good Shepherd in the Bible. We are likened to sheep. He loves us like a shepherd loves his sheep, and He tenderly cares for us." I told them about one day in Pakistan when I sat on my back steps, which overlooked a green valley in the Himalayan mountains. I saw a shepherd who sat all day looking after one sheep. I could not believe he would spend all day watching carefully over only one sheep, rather than a large herd of them. I shared how I heard the Spirit of God say to me, *Joy, that is how I am. You are My beloved lamb, and I look after you tenderly, as if you are the only sheep in the whole world*. Mohammed and Fatima were visibly moved by the analogy.

The candy cane analogy is a wonderful way to help make the truths of the Gospel clear to Muslims who are hearing it for the first time.

I then continued with my candy cane analogy. "Now if you turn the candy cane upside down it looks like a *J*, which stands for Jesus," I demonstrated. That fascinated them. I went on, "If you put two candy canes together, they form a heart, like the heart of God that is full of love for you. Jesus loves you, Mohammed and Fatima."

My heart was singing by this time. I had the privilege of telling this Muslim family that Jesus loves them. What other prophet could we say loves us? Certainly not Moses or Noah or Abraham. It gave me such joy to reveal God's love to them that I could have floated out of there!

Handing the candy canes to Mohammed and Fatima, I asked if they could tell the story back to me. It was thrilling for them, and because it was visual it was easy for them to explain it even in their minimal English.

The candy cane analogy is a wonderful way to help make the truths of the Gospel clear to Muslims who are hearing it for the first time. The analogy, however, is not always received with such joy. One Christmas Day we invited a number of refugee children and youth to our home for a big feast. Afterward we shared the Gospel with them through the candy cane symbolism. I asked which one would like to tell it back to us. The young man who seemed the most resistant to the Gospel volunteered. We were amazed that he got the whole Gospel account correct. By the time Christmas arrived the following year, however, the same youth had entered a treacherous underground world of gangs and drugs, and seeing the candy canes in a store tempted him to break them all!

Easter

Muslims all over the world have heard the word *Christmas*. *Easter*, however, is less known and understood.

Afsana called me one Easter to wish me "Happy Bunny's Day!" It sounded so cute the way she said it. I laughed and asked where she had picked that up. Her English language teacher had informed Afsana's class that they should wish everyone a "Happy Bunny's Day." Often such teachers are the first to introduce new cultural information to their eager students, who listen carefully to their teachers and esteem them highly. Fortunate is the Muslim student who sits under the teaching and influence of a Christian who is not afraid to inform them of Christian facts in a sensitive manner.

"Afsana, did your teacher tell you what holiday it actually is?" I inquired.

"No. What is Bunny's Day?" I took the opportunity to explain to Afsana the account of Jesus, and she was surprised that it did not have anything to do with bunnies. She listened carefully and respectfully while I disclosed that the holiday was actually the hugely significant Christian celebration of Jesus' death and resurrection. Afsana was upset that it had been kept from her.

Abdi had not heard such confusing stories of Easter. He came to know about Easter in a mysterious way. He had a strange dream in which a man in a white robe came to him and touched his forehead, saying, "Abdi, wake up. It is Easter."

He awoke startled and nudged his wife in bed. "Layla, do you know what Easter is?"

"No," she said groggily.

Later that day Abdi asked numerous people if they knew what Easter was, but they were not able to help him. He called our home, and I answered the phone. It was both shocking and thrilling to hear a Muslim ask me, "Joy, do you know what Easter is?"

"Of course, Abdi, I know about Easter," I assured him. "Would you like me to come to your home and explain it to you?" His curiosity was piqued, and he was determined to find out. I could hardly wait! I soon arrived at the home of a Muslim couple who were eager and anxious to hear the meaning of this dream. I took great pleasure in unfolding the mysterious dream that had left them dangling in suspense. I felt at home that day with Abdi and Layla.

Abdi went on to tell numerous people about his exciting dream and its interpretation. The Holy Spirit has amazing and endless ways of communicating truth.

The Importance of the Christmas and Easter Accounts

The Christmases of my childhood years in Somalia, an Islamic country, were simple and noncommercialized. I did not have to contend with any confusion such as Muslims in the West experience. The Church had just been born in this area for the first time in the history of the world. The Somali Bible had not yet been completed, and it was exhilarating to read some of the first Scripture verses of the Christmas story to Somali men and women in their native language at house church celebrations. The birth of Jesus Christ was an auspicious and noteworthy occasion to celebrate.

We Christians need to remember the noteworthiness of these holidays and the importance of communicating that to our Muslim friends. The Christmas and Easter accounts are the heart of Christianity, and they provide a wonderful way to give Muslims the Gospel account.

10

On Display

We have spent wonderful times with Muslims both in our home and in their homes. It seems as if almost everything significant takes place in homes. We decided long ago to open our home with hospitality to these strangers in our land. We pray that by doing so they will learn to feel more at home with us. Sometimes, however, it has felt as if our home were on display and my husband and I were the tour guides.

A Look Inside

Muslims visiting our home often make me think of the time Ed and I visited Notre Dame Basilica in Montreal, Quebec. One of our Iranian friends had toured the cathedral and urged us to see it while we were in Montreal. He also had sent us a package of Iranian postcards depicting impressive historical churches in Iran.

Tourists from around the world were lined up, curious to see the inside of this cathedral built in 1829. I had never been in a cathedral before, and Notre Dame did not fit my preconceived ideas. I never expected it to look so extravagant or ornate. I marveled at the gorgeous stained-glass windows, gold-tipped polychrome carvings, paintings, statues, lavish altar, impressive organ and big bell. I was awed by the quietness and respect tourists showed as they surveyed everything on display. Some even stopped at the altar and knelt to pray or lit a candle. Obviously the grandeur and beauty of that cathedral affected all of us.

There is something intriguing about seeing a cathedral, famous building or show home. People are intensely curious about what a building looks like on the inside. We are not satisfied to simply read about it or see it from the outside. We want to look inside for ourselves.

Muslims visiting our home often are curious about what is inside. Most have never been inside a Christian home and, just as I felt before entering the cathedral, they do not know what to expect. Our goal is to ensure that Jesus is on display in our home so that He can touch their hearts.

Halim and Sakina Visit Our Home

One evening in particular Ed and I felt as if our home were on display. Halim and Sakina, along with their two children, had come to our home for the first time. Having never been in a Christian home before, they were thrilled with our invitation and quite curious. It was as if they were the tourists and we were the guides, and we and our home were on display.

Before coming, they nervously informed us they did not eat pig or drink alcohol because those things are forbidden (*haram*) in the Qur'an. We assured them we would not serve them either one. I could hear their sigh of relief. *Poor people,* I thought. *They wanted to come but were anxious about what they would do if pork or alcohol was served, and they did not want to embarrass or offend us by declining in front of us.* I had learned years earlier that food could be an extremely sensitive issue for conservative Muslims. Once I had served Rice Krispie squares to a Muslim family for dessert. As they were eating them, the wife asked how I made them. When I mentioned marshmallows, she immediately told her children to go throw the squares in the garbage and spit out the food. She was afraid the marshmallows had gelatin in them. Gelatin can be made from pig bones, making it prohibited under Islamic law. Eating it would bring them under the stern punishment of Allah.

Halim and Sakina came from the upper echelon of their society, and I wondered what they would think of our simple home. Some of our Muslim friends who have come from a high-class background find it difficult to associate with lower income people. Culturally speaking, we understand their struggle, as many facets of our society and culture have strikingly contrasting values and expectations. Halim and Sakina, however, graciously accepted our invitation and arrived with a box of chocolates as a hostess gift, believing a guest should never come to someone's home empty-handed.

We seated them in the living room, offering toys to their children. Everyone was a little shy in the beginning. Though they were thrilled and honored, they understandably felt a bit uncomfortable, as this was a new experience for them. I busied myself in the kitchen preparing the last-minute touches to the meal of rice, barbecued fish, meatballs and salad. I asked Sakina to join me in the kitchen and motioned for her to take a seat.

She was quiet, not knowing what to talk about. I knew what she wanted more than anything else, and it was not to talk. I knew she wanted a tour of our house, as most of our friends desire, for then she would be able to relax and feel more at home. So before we gathered at the table for our meal, I offered her a chance to see our home.

Keenly inquisitive, Sakina observed everything with great interest: the curtains, furniture, pictures and wedding photos, knickknacks on the shelves, beds and even the sheets and blankets. I answered many questions—talk about a tour guide! Later that evening Sakina told Halim she wanted to take pictures of some of the wall hangings, knickknacks and plaques with religious words that meant something to her. Sakina wanted to remember their visit, just as we had wanted to remember our visit inside that cathedral and had taken pictures of it. Our home was on display.

Our Evening Together

Ed and I had decided to sit at the table to eat. Sometimes our Muslim friends feel more at home eating on the floor with a plastic tablecloth on the carpet, depending upon which country they come from. But we felt Halim and Sakina would be comfortable enough sitting on chairs at our table.

I could see they were starting to talk more freely and feeling more relaxed by the time we gathered at the table. Before we started dishing out the food, we explained to them that our custom was to first thank God for our food, if they did not mind. They did not understand fully what we meant by praying before we ate, but Ed went ahead and thanked God for the food and asked a blessing upon our guests. That prayer was the first Christian prayer Halim and Sakina had ever heard, and it was their first concrete introduction to a Christian home. We continued to try to make them feel at home as we talked about our families, which put them at ease.

Then at the end of the meal they watched in amazement as Ed helped clear the dishes and asked me if I needed any more help. Definite impressions were being absorbed.

After the meal I asked Sakina if she would like to sit in the living room with the men and talk or if she wanted to be with the children. She preferred the latter, leaving Ed and Halim in the living room. Sakina felt most at home being apart from the men.

Halim had noticed our shelf of books in different languages and inquired about them. They are Bibles in different languages, which sparked his curiosity. He had never handled or read a Bible. From childhood he had been told by Muslim clerics at the mosques that it had been changed and that the Qur'an superseded it as the final truth, and he had never considered checking out whether that statement was true or not. Ed asked him if he would like to hear some words Jesus said. That got Halim's attention because he believed in Jesus and respected Him as an esteemed prophet. Ed read Matthew 5:1–10 (the Beatitudes), which sparked an animated conversation between the two of them for the next hour.

In the meantime, Sakina and I were in another room where the children could play with toys. I sat for a while with the children on the couch, reading silly stories to them and enjoying the sounds of their delightful giggles. Seeing her children snuggled up to me listening to the stories made Sakina feel that her children had a grandmother. She regretted her children not having her mother nearby. They later drew pictures for me, which I hung on my kitchen art wall.

Eid al Adha, the religious festival that commemorates the time when, according to the Qur'an, Abraham attempted to sacrifice Ishmael, was going to be celebrated the next week in their Islamic community. Anticipation and religious fervor of the momentous celebration was in the air. Many Muslims were performing the *Hajj* pilgrimage in Mecca at that very time. "What will you do for *Eid*, Sakina?" I asked her.

"Halim will go with some of our Muslim friends to the Hutterite farm and kill a sheep," Sakina replied. "We will eat that and go to the mosque for special prayers on *Eid*. And there will be some big parties next weekend. But it never feels like *Eid* here like it does back home." Sakina's voice and eyes reflected a sadness and longing to be with her family in her country. "There we give some of our sheep meat to the poor and all the schools and offices are closed."

I wanted to find out if Sakina understood the true history of Abraham's willingness to sacrifice his beloved son. I explained to her that while the Qur'an states that son is Ishmael, in the biblical account he is Isaac. As we pursued the history and spiritual meaning, it became clear that Sakina had little understanding of the deep spiritual implications of the commemoration, nor of the beginnings of Judaism. Like most Muslims, Sakina believed Abraham (*Ibrahim*) was a famous Muslim prophet. She became interested when I explained how Abraham was called out of Ur by Jehovah God to inherit a land that would be given to him. She looked somewhat confused when I began to explain about Sarah and Isaac, as Hagar and Ishmael were much more familiar to her. Our discussion went on a long time, her eyes showing both bewilderment and surprise as I unfolded the historical record of Israel and the Jews. "I never knew all that!" Sakina exclaimed.

"I never knew all that!" Sakina exclaimed.

"I know, Sakina. A lot of Muslims do not understand how the whole historical picture fits together chronologically. It helps to understand what is happening in the world today if the history is clear," I explained.

Superstition and Curses

The subject changed to the upcoming birth of her baby. It made her comfortable talking about her pregnancy.

"I play tapes of the Qur'an every day close to my womb, so my baby can be directly affected by the hearing of it," she disclosed to me. "And I have a little Qur'an in the baby's crib, too."

"Why do you do that, Sakina?" I asked. I knew as soon as her baby was born somebody would breathe an Islamic blessing into his ear ensuring protection over the baby and celebrating that another Muslim had been born into the world.

"Well, my mother told me I should do that to make sure everything will turn out okay because I must have a C-section this time, but also so my baby will come into the world loving Islam."

"That's called superstition, Sakina. Do you know what superstition is?"

"No. What's that?" she asked, never having heard the word before. I had previously observed that Sakina, like many Muslim women, held quite a few superstitious beliefs. Once she had given me a photo of Amira, her daughter, dressed like a boy to ward off the evil eye. And once she insisted I drink the whole glass of orange juice she served me to prevent something bad happening to my husband. Another time I sneezed twice, and she was relieved it had not been just one time because that meant something ominous would happen.

Superstition is part of the Muslim culture. Their superstitions and fears originate from the ways they view God and themselves.

Superstition is part of the Muslim culture. Their superstitions and fears originate from the ways they view God and themselves. To them God is personally unknowable and able to do what He wants. To the Muslim woman God is the Master and she is the slave, not His child, as the Bible teaches. She believes that if He wants to bless and forgive her, then He will. If He wants to punish her, then He will. If He wants her to go to heaven, then He will ensure she goes there. She views God as quick to punish, which produces in her the fruit of fear. She never knows for certain if God is "for her" or "against her." She perceives herself as helpless, but she does what she can to gain God's favor, appease His anger and ward off His punishment and judgments. Her dominant fears revolve around the evil eye, *jinn* and Satan, hell and death and being punished by Allah. Her fear of *jinn*, which she believes are either good or evil supernatural beings created out of fire, can make her feel unprotected. Her view of God is not based on the biblical attributes of Jehovah God's love, mercy and justice. The thought of God loving her and thus protecting her is not based on the character of God, but on her ability to do good deeds and be faithful to His commands. On top of all this, she is a fatalist, convinced that whatever takes place is according to luck or fate. Sakina's fear and superstition provided a good opportunity to share the protection that is found in Jesus.

"Well, Sakina, when people are afraid of the possibility of something bad happening we sometimes try to take some measure of control into our own hands, and we invent ways to divert bad luck from happening. That is called superstition. People do all sorts of superstitious things to bring about blessing, success or good luck. Sometimes women wear necklaces with verses from the Qur'an inscribed on them for protection, just like some people wear crosses for that reason. Sometimes people put up verses from the Qur'an on their walls not just as a declaration of faith or a blessing, but for protection. I have seen eye symbols pinned to babies' clothes to keep the eye of bad *jinn* from harming them. You know, Sakina, I have been in Muslim homes where the women are afraid of being alone so they put on recitation recordings of the Qur'an, thinking that somehow the chanting will protect them from Satan or *jinn*. People do these things, Sakina, because they fear God and worry that He will use His power to harm them. But the Bible teaches that God does not want to harm us because He loves us very much. It says God is for us, not against us, and that He is jealous over us with a pure, good jealousy. It is sometimes hard to believe that God, who is almighty in power, is so totally good and full of love."

"Well, that's just our culture. I do not know why we do those things. It is just our culture," she answered. I could see that this was heavy on her heart because she wanted to ensure that everything turn out well with her baby. Sakina then began to disclose her deep concern for her sister back home, whom she felt had had a curse put on her. She looked at me with a resigned, hopeless feeling, wondering if I would understand because nobody ever talked about curses in her new homeland. I decided to share a story with her about a woman I encountered at the mission hospital in Pakistan years earlier.

"Sakina, I understand your concern." She looked relieved. "There was a young, beautiful woman admitted to our mission hospital in Pakistan, and she looked quite ill. Her mother-in-law always sat hawkeyed by her bedside. One day as I walked past her hospital bed, a Pakistani Christian nurse took me aside and said, 'You know, Joy, there is nothing really wrong with her.' Well, it did not look that way to me, but who was I to say, not being a medical expert? I decided to step into a quiet room and offer a simple prayer asking Jesus to help the suffering patient. I soon found the woman sitting up in bed looking completely normal." Relaying the story to Sakina, I recalled how shocked I had felt. How could that happen? What happened? This was all new territory for me.

Sakina was fully engrossed in my story. She had no problem understanding.

"And Sakina," I continued, "as I spoke with the transformed young woman, she confided in me that her husband had rejected her. So his mother had taken her to a local person who claimed to have special powers. She was given a piece of paper with a verse from the Qur'an on it and told to eat it. The mother-in-law believed this would make her daughter-in-law go crazy, and then she could get rid of her. I told the transformed patient, 'When I heard there was nothing really physically wrong with you, I suspected that it was more spiritual in nature, such as a curse put on you, so I went off to pray for you and simply asked Jesus to help you.' I explained to her that Jesus had made her well. She looked so peaceful and happy! I later spoke with her mother-in-law and explained that what she had done was *haram* and God was not pleased at all. She listened carefully as I read verses to her from the Bible about using sorcery on someone."

Sakina was all ears, as she was terrified of evil spirits that could harm her. I offered to pray for her and her sister, clarifying that I myself had no power at all but that the name of Jesus has all power over Satan, *jinn*, curses or anything else that we fear.

Faith on Display

As we were talking, Halim came into the room and said they should be going. As they were preparing to leave, the children ran over to the piano and began touching it, amazed at the sounds that came out of it. I asked them if they would like to hear a special song. Seeing their delighted response, I sat down and played "God Is So Good," making up new verses such as "God Loves Amira" for the sake of the three-year-old.

Soon we all were gathered around the piano singing "God Is So Good." Halim and Sakina and their children observed true worship on display for the first time.

They thanked us profusely for the evening, repeatedly saying they wanted to return the invitation and have us visit their home. Before they left, Ed asked if we could pray for the upcoming birth of their baby. They agreed and were deeply touched as they observed prayer on display.

Indeed our faith was on display. Our furniture, wall plaques, marriage, the way we honored them as guests, our table grace, the words from the Bible, our faith in God sprinkled throughout the conversations, our worship of God through the simple medium of a children's chorus and our farewell benediction blessing over them left them with a clearer understanding of what it means to be a Christian. Though we wanted to serve them a delicious meal and honor them with hospitality, our primary goal was to honor our Chief Guest, the Lord Jesus Christ. We wanted Him to be on display within our home. Above all we desired to reach their hearts.

Though we wanted to serve them a delicious meal and honor them with hospitality, our primary goal was to honor our Chief Guest, the Lord Jesus Christ.

The Houses of Their Lives

When it comes to reaching Muslims, I often think of a house surrounded by a wall and a locked gate. A guard is on duty, limiting access. In the same way, it is not always easy to gain access into the lives and hearts of Muslims. They can have many locked doors and guarded gates, such as fear, resistance or ignorance. Halim and Sakina, for example, initially had been afraid of coming to our home for fear that we might serve them pork or alcohol. But God has the power to unlock the doors and keep them open. The Holy Spirit makes it possible for us to be welcomed and invited into the houses of their lives.

Just as our home and lives were on display for Halim and Sakina on that delightful evening, we continued a relationship with them and, with their permission, we walked through the house of their lives. First we were invited into the "kitchen," where we talked about ethnic foods and recipes—light talk. We enjoyed relating on this level for some time, but we wanted to move into other rooms of Halim and Sakina's lives.

As we moved from talking about trivial things in the "kitchen," we ventured into the "living room" space of their lives, where we talked more about their lives and community. We then began to move into the "family room," where the conversations deepened as they opened up about some of the problems and struggles they were facing. With some other Muslim friends we have been taken into the "bathroom," where arguments and disagreements about topics like politics have exploded vehemently, and we have had to cut our visit short. Fortunately, in the case of Halim and Sakina, those kinds of unprofitable topics did not arise. For some time, Sakina and I went into the "basement," where the spiritual needs of her soul, with its secret fears and superstitions, were exposed. I tried to take her to the cross, where Jesus could bear her guilt, fear and shame. I did not want to stay in the "basement," however. I wanted to take her out to the "deck" into the sunshine of the light of Jesus.

We did not bang hard on the doors of their lives. We did not barge in. That would not have made them feel at home; it would have made them want to run. No, we knocked gently but persistently, as Jesus knocks. "Look! I stand at the door and knock. If you hear my voice and open the door, I will come in, and we will share a meal together as friends" (Revelation 3:20).

The gospel accounts reveal Jesus in the homes of many people. In homes He evangelized, taught, healed and restored. In homes He was honored with banquets and feasts, worshiped and even anointed once by a sinful, repentant woman. In homes He disclosed the secrets of His Kingdom and revealed His glory. After His resurrection He appeared and disappeared in spite of closed doors. So many significant events happened in homes when Jesus graced them with His ministry of love and compassion. He did not have an office. He ministered where people were most comfortable. Likewise, the treasures and secrets of Jesus Christ are often best revealed and explained to Muslims in the privacy of our homes, rather than in a public arena. When Jesus is on display in our homes, hearts are touched.

11

The "Gentleman"

The day I met Husna most of her beauty was hidden under a loose-fitting cloak and *hijab*. Her skin color was so light that I had to look twice to believe she was not Caucasian. Her lovely eyes, like shiny marbles, and her chiseled bone structure conveyed an aura of royalty. In minimal English and a shy, quiet voice she asked if I would come to her home to help her learn English. I was delighted.

"Welcome, Joy," Husna said with a warm smile as she ushered me into her home for the first time. We gave each other the customary Eastern kisses on both cheeks. Was this really the same woman I had met earlier? She looked considerably different without her *hijab* and cloak, which had so effectively hidden her beauty. Dressed in jeans and a top, she was stunning. It never fails to amaze me how a long cloak and head covering can dramatically transform a woman's appearance. Like most Westerners, I used to find it more difficult to feel at home with a Muslim woman when she is dressed in her Islamic garb, even though she is the same person. Today the garb does not loom as noticeably to me. Nevertheless, dressing alike does give us common ground.

As Husna prepared tea with homemade cake and fresh fruit, I looked around her living room. Husna had good taste. Her home was immaculate—more so than mine! The smell of pungent incense wafted through the air, and I knew she had burned it to show me honor. Her hospitable character, keen fashion sense and lovely home décor all conveyed an elegant beauty not often seen in our culture. She reminded me of Queen Esther in the Bible—so much so that I later lent her a movie about Esther. Yet this regal, elegant Muslim beauty, like so many other Muslim women, was struggling under harshness and punishment. She longed for gentleness.

Husna's Struggle

One day as we chatted Husna began showing me family photos. She carefully selected one and showed it to me so cautiously that it seemed something about it was illegal. The photo showed her without her *hijab*. "I cannot have my photo taken without my *hijab*," she confided.

"Why, Husna?" I asked gently. The door to the home of her heart slowly and cautiously opened.

"Asif would get jealous and angry," she said sadly. "He also tells me what I can or cannot wear." I could tell the *hijab* was an issue of contention in their home, and the picture of Asif that she conveyed was not that of a gentleman.

I showed her a photo from my days in Pakistan in which I wore a large *chadar* cloth. "Is that really you, Joy?" she asked incredulously.

"Yes, it is. No law dictated that I wear a *chadar*, but I wore it so I would not give men the idea I was a Hollywood woman," I explained. "Sometimes in the marketplace I would actually pull it over my face if I saw men staring at me too much. I really did not have any problem with wearing it. I got used to it. One thing I know, Husna, is that wearing a *hijab* or a *chadar* may cover our bodies, but it does not cover our hearts. God looks at what is in our hearts. We can have selfishness, jealousy, lying, deceit, gossip, feelings of revenge or cursing, and a *hijab* does not get rid of those things. I have talked with many Muslim women who think that wearing a *hijab* makes them acceptable before God or in some way pleases Him. But actually, Husna, the Bible says that there is nothing we can do, no matter how hard we try, to make us acceptable before God. But there is a way to become acceptable to God. May I share that with you, Husna?"

Little by little I began unfolding the story of redemption, starting with Adam and Eve and culminating with the sacrifice of Jesus on the cross. "It is the blood of Jesus Christ shed on the cross for our sins that makes us right and acceptable before God. You see, Jesus Christ has provided the way and the means. We can either accept God's way or reject it. All over the world people try to determine ways to please God, but God has determined only one way. We try to pray faithfully, give money to the poor or even fast.

Husna longed for a husband who would treat her like a gentleman.

"Those are good things, but they cannot make us acceptable before God. Trusting in the blood of Jesus is such a liberating truth. Because I trust in that, Husna, I know I am accepted by God. I do not need to wear a *hijab*." I wanted her to understand that no human effort could make us acceptable or pleasing to God. A *hijab* may create a human acceptance within a community, but it cannot make us spiritually pleasing to the Lord. Only the sacrificial blood of Jesus makes us spiritually acceptable to Him.

"You are complete, Joy," she concluded.

"Yes, I am, Husna. Jesus has made me complete. It makes me happy and at peace." Her conclusion surprised me in its simple truth. I had never heard a Muslim woman say such a thing. I only wished she could feel that way about herself.

As our relationship grew, Husna, my beautiful, cheerful friend, slowly began to lose her happy spirit. As she confided in me, I learned that her marriage was difficult. She longed for a husband who would treat her like a gentleman. Day by day she sank into deeper depression. She missed her family. Finally, unable to bear her loneliness any longer, she returned to her country to visit her family for a month. I thought she would return revitalized, but nothing really changed.

Shortly after her return I noticed she was not wearing the *hijab* anymore. "What happened, Husna?" I asked. "You are not wearing the *hijab*."

She replied, "I told Asif that this is a free country. Women have their rights, and I have decided not to wear the *hijab*. He is giving me a terrible time. We have lots of fights about it. He began hitting me."

I did not know what to say. I prayed for wisdom. Twenty years earlier I would have dealt swiftly with such a situation but not always wisely. I sought guidance from the Holy Spirit and asked my Emergency Prayer Community for counsel. Occasionally when Muslim women immigrate to the West they stop wearing the *hijab*. That is not a problem if their husbands comply with that. But Husna's husband was not in agreement and had become violent.

A few days later I visited a teahouse and saw a creative piece of work that made me think of women like Husna who feel abused or controlled. It was a Christmas tree decorated with cracked or chipped china teacups hanging from the branches. I bought one of those teacups for Husna.

"Husna, here is a special gift picked just for you," I said, handing her the package during our next visit together.

"Oh," she exclaimed. "It is beautiful! I love you." She came over and kissed me on the cheek.

"I love you, too, my dear friend. There's a special meaning behind the china cup." I told her about the Christmas tree. "Instantly I thought of you, Husna, and some of my other friends, too. You and those other women remind me of beautiful china teacups that have been cracked. To me the Christmas tree I saw was symbolic of many women who have been broken and wounded and yet remain beautiful treasures."

For many Muslim women, the gentleness of Jesus is what draws them like a magnet. Gentleness is irresistibly powerful! Husna, who was more accustomed to harshness, pain, guilt and shame, recognized the gentleness of Jesus, and this was what attracted her to Him. She loved to hear about Christ, particularly biblical accounts such as the adulterous woman whom Jesus rescued from being stoned or the woman who had bled for so long and finally was healed when she touched Jesus' garment. I am always eager to read such biblical accounts of Jesus' gentleness to Husna and other Muslim women, as their responses are so precious.

For many Muslim women, the gentleness of Jesus is what draws them like a magnet.

When I share Jesus in this way with them, I often feel His gentle presence washing over them and pouring into their homes like a refreshing breeze. I love to share the message with them that Jesus does not discard women who are broken. Rather, He preserves them as treasures. I want them to know that they have high value in His eyes!

Jamila

The sky was clear blue with no clouds in sight the day I met Jamila—a perfect day to visit our favorite city park. Boys kicked a soccer ball. Kurdish men smoked and discussed politics, judging by their raised voices. Somali women in their bright, loose cotton dresses talked animatedly with each other or on their cell phones while their children played on the swings and slide. Muslim women, clad in their cloaks and *hijabs*, crisscrossed the paths. This park is a drawing place for newcomers from many countries. I feel at home here.

Jesus does not discard women who are broken. Rather, He preserves them as treasures.

That afternoon as my husband and I walked through the park we noticed a Muslim couple sitting on a bench watching their children play on the nearby playground. We began chatting with them and soon discovered they were newly arrived from the Middle East. They were unusually friendly and responsive. They were curious about the big church across from the park.

"You are always welcome to visit the church," we offered.

"My wife, Jamila, would like to visit, if you do not mind," the man spoke for her.

"That's great. We will pick you up at 10:30 A.M. on Sunday." We exchanged phone numbers and got their address.

When we arrived to pick her up, Jamila was dressed in her black *abaya* cloak and large black headscarf. We wondered how this experience would be for her. Church does not always feel like home for a Muslim woman when she first enters. Everything is strange and new. People might stare at her. She is not used to musical instruments, as there is no music in a mosque. The praying is different. Everyone is sitting on a chair or pew, rather than on the floor, and men and women sit together—even on the same pew with their bodies nearly touching one another. And they wear shoes, unlike Muslims, who leave their shoes outside the door. The little cups of juice and small bits of cracker are unusual to them. But in spite of all of this, Jamila was a good sport. She plunged right in and tried to sing the worship songs, lifting her hands like many others were doing. When people around her said hallelujah, she joined them. When people went forward for prayer, Jamila started crying. She found that part of the service inviting and gentle. She wiped away her tears with her *hijab*. I put my arm around her but did not say anything because I sensed that the Holy Spirit was sweeping over her, ministering gently to her soul.

Jamila came to church with us again. And on her third visit she whipped off her black scarf and stated loudly and exuberantly, "Freedom! I love Jesus!"

Surprised at her childlike outburst of joy, I asked, "Why do you love Jesus?"

"Jesus, gentleman!"

How true! Jesus is gentle and kind, and Jamila had discovered that wonderful truth.

Jesus, who was both fully man and fully God, was an exemplary gentleman when it came to His manhood. He was pure, sinless and the only perfect man to walk this earth. Frequently a Muslim woman has to process the model of Jesus' manhood before she can move further to His deity. The men in Jamila's life could be harsh, and she sometimes withered under it. Thankfully Jamila's husband did not stop her growing interest in Christ. He actually seemed relieved that her attention was on religious things.

One day Jamila pulled up her dress to show me black and blue marks. I addressed her husband. "Jamal, you know that is *haram* (forbidden). You must not hit your wife." As a respected middle-aged woman, I could get away with giving such instruction to him. In Islam, so unlike our Western culture that idolizes youth, the older a woman becomes, the greater respect she is given.

Experiencing Harshness

Unfortunately in some Muslim families, beatings such as Husna and Jamila received are not uncommon. I know Muslim women who have seldom known gentleness and mercy, but rather have withered under harshness and punishment. I have seen scars of burns or stab wounds on bodies that cry out for comfort and compassion, broken fingers left unset, eyesight lost from a beating or teeth knocked out. I have seen pressure put on teenage daughters to become slim, potential candidates for marriage that has caused them to become anorexic or bulimic.

I know of a woman and her toddler who were imprisoned in a Middle Eastern country for suspicion of associating with a certain political group. She endured torture, and her young child was released to wander the streets. I have known Muslim women who have been haunted by memories of female genital mutilation. I have taken care of babies of unmarried girls who have been raped, often by a male relative. I have seen young girls who have worked like slaves cooking and cleaning. I have seen brokenhearted young women forced to marry someone they did not love and married women who have been forced by their husbands to become pregnant. I have seen others controlled by mothers-in-law. I have seen punitive husbands confiscate or destroy cherished photos of family members or hide passports. While certainly Christians and people of all faiths can be guilty of these same sins, all of these incidents I mention represent Muslim women whom

I know personally. Because of their experiences, kindness, grace, mercy and gentleness speak loudly to them and draw them like a magnet.

Drawn by Christ's Gentleness

Because many Muslim women have experienced harshness, pain and loss, the gentleness of Jesus appeals to them. They feel at home when they sense gentleness. Militancy, loudness and dogmatism make them want to run.

This is especially important to remember when we are sharing the truths of Jesus with Muslim women. Sometimes we are passionate about our faith, but if we are not careful, we can bowl them over. If we do not take care to maintain a gentle relationship with them or if we become adversarial in our delivery, our attempt is counterproductive. They are weary of fear and control tactics, especially from authority figures who exert religious power. Muslim women often have never heard biblical truths. Sharing those truths with them in a gentle, kind, caring spirit can go a long way in helping them process new information. Indeed the candle of Christ's gentleness and kindness can shine into any darkness.

The candle of Christ's gentleness and kindness can shine into any darkness.

In the journey of life it is the cry of every human heart to receive unconditional mercy, grace, gentleness and kindness. When we have been touched by these virtues we want to freely dispense them toward others. Yes, as Husna and Jamila and countless other Muslim women have discovered, Jesus is indeed a "gentleman."

12

Babies

Muslim women believe that their core significance, or worth, is found in producing babies, preferably sons. Motherhood is highly esteemed, and so it should be. We would do well to learn more of that value from Muslims. For Arab women, motherhood is such a high honor that they take great pleasure in being addressed as *Um Hamid* ("mother of my son, Hamid" or whatever her son's name is)—even more than by their own name. Rather than seeing themselves through the eyes of God and knowing they are loved by Him, Muslim women find their highest value in being a mother. I learned this truth from two pregnant Muslim women.

Amina

"Is your son's wife pregnant?" Amina asked, not thinking it an inappropriate question. Amina, typical of many of my Muslim friends, is intensely interested in every detail of my children and grandchildren's lives. Most of the time her interest endears her to me. It makes me feel like we are one big family. When sickness or difficulty arises in my family, she becomes concerned. She wants to enter into the joys and sorrows of engagements, weddings, pregnancies, births and deaths of my family, and she wants me to enter into those events in her life as well. After my daughter had her first baby, Amina asked me to take her to visit. She cradled baby Emily in her loving brown arms as if she were the proud auntie. I have learned a lot about the importance of family cohesiveness from Muslim women.

But this time I replied with some discomfort to my friend's inquiry. "I do not know, Amina."

"How about your daughter?" she persisted.

"She is happy with her two children," I answered, hoping the discussion would end there. But unsatisfied, Amina replied, "Only two children? We like to have lots. It is my job. I get lots of money from the government." No doubt about that. Muslim families from Amina's people group often have up to ten children, allowing them to receive a sizable family allowance check from our government every month for each child under eighteen years old. Amina clearly believed that the more children a mother birthed, the greater her worth.

Amina had arrived in Canada single. A refugee, she did not have much family support in place, as most of them were in refugee camps. After a year of helping Amina with practical needs every refugee faces and walking with her through a season of depression, I noticed that she seemed unusually cheerful. A Muslim man she had met in her refugee camp, also newly arrived in our country, had just proposed to her. A romance had budded in a refugee camp! I was intrigued that something as mysterious and delightful as a romance could develop in a place known for such deplorable conditions.

The following weeks were full of excitement and anticipation as the wedding plans fell into place. Amina had arrived in our country wearing no *hijab*, but now it became part of her attire. With it she was announcing that she was becoming a married woman, much like Westerners wear engagement rings. It was a simple wedding. Two new refugees on government assistance did not have much money. But they were happy and in love. It was an honor to share in their wedding.

But Amina did not live with Omar the first few weeks after they got married, and this confused me. "Are you actually married, Amina?" I asked. "Why are you not living with Omar?"

"I had an operation, Joy," she told me. She explained she had had reconstructive surgery for the female circumcision performed when she was a young girl. It was taking time to heal. I shuddered at the thought. A short time later, she proudly announced, "Joy, I am pregnant! Pray I will have a boy."

"I am so happy for you, Amina. Congratulations! But why do you want me to pray you will have a boy?" I probed.

"My people like to have boys—lots of them," she answered. "We like girls, too, but we want boys first."

"So boys are preferred to girls?"

"Yaah," she replied. I loved the way Amina responded often with a long, drawn-out *yaah*. It endeared her to me and made me feel at home with her. Amina was easy to love.

"How does that make you feel, Amina, since you are female? Did you feel that your brothers were more special than you growing up?" I questioned her.

"We just get used to it," she answered with a quiet resignation.

"Pray for Me, Joy"

Amina was terrified of labor and delivery. She had heard horror stories of women suffering in childbirth as a result of female genital mutilation. "Pray for me, Joy," she begged over and over again. Seeing her great fear and anxiety, I would lay my hand on her growing abdomen and in the name of Jesus ask God for a smooth delivery. Knowing that Muslims believe Jesus has healing powers but vehemently deny He is God, I wanted Amina to understand clearly who Jesus is. I have learned that it is important that Muslims understand who Jesus really is when I pray for them.

"He is more than a healing prophet, Amina," I said, trying to help her understand. "The Qu'ran states many times that Jesus is a prophet and did many healing miracles. But the Bible says that Jesus is more than a prophet. Jesus was God who came into our world in the appearance of a human being.

I have learned that it is important that Muslims understand who Jesus really is when I pray for them.

"He came from heaven to earth. A man did not become God; God became a human being. And He was born from the virgin Mary. That has never happened to anyone else in history. We call him Jesus, or *Isa al Masih*." Though this was a far-out revelation to her, Amina did not respond in the typical argumentative way, so I continued. "Do you know why?"

"No," she replied, confused but curious to know more about such a foreign concept. The conversation was moving along spiritually, so I pressed a bit further.

"There are a lot of problems in the world, aren't there? Do you know why we have problems in the world?" She hadn't thought about it before. I took her back to Adam and Eve, who were created perfect but chose to disobey God in the Garden. I explained that as a result of that choice sin entered the world, and consequently, we are all born with the desire to sin. I explained that Adam and Eve's sin caused something like a spiritual divorce between God and them.

"Do you know the difference between separation and divorce, Amina?" I asked. "When a husband and wife separate, their marriage is not necessarily over. In your culture when a husband and wife have problems, the wife can go to her family's home for a period of time and negotiations can be made. That is separation. Often you get back together after negotiating. But if a divorce happens, everyone knows the marriage is finished. Well, God was angry with Adam and Eve. He had told them that if they ate that fruit they would die. The sacred friendship between God and them would be over. They chose to take that forbidden fruit, so God had to punish their sin. They were banished from their home and from the presence of God. But, Amina, God is so full of love that He made another way for Adam and Eve and all people to come back home into that wonderful sacred friendship with Him. God in His great love knew how He could fix the divorce between Himself and sinful people. He Himself came into the world in the appearance of Jesus to make that possible. He gave His life to take away our sin and bring us back together. That is what the story of the cross is all about. It's all about the deep love of God for us. We can find a new home in Jesus.

"People all over the world are trying to become acceptable to God, Amina. We try all kinds of ways to make that happen. But we by ourselves cannot become acceptable to Him. God sent prophets into the world to explain God's laws and guidance, but the laws, even though they are good, cannot make us acceptable or right with God—just like reading a book on how to drive a car cannot make you a perfect driver. No, we needed Jesus' death on the cross to end the divorce and restore our relationship with Him.

"Amina, God never wanted us to be divorced from Him. He loves us! And He loved us so much that He made a way for us to be reconciled to Him. He loved us so much that He gave His own life for us. That is true love, Amina. And that is how much we are worth to Him."

Amina had wanted me to pray for her baby, which I did, but her request gave me the opportunity to explain to her that her greatest worth is not found in being a mother. I knew that Amina could understand her true worth only when she understands how much God loves her. With the help and leading of the Holy Spirit I was able to plant a seed in Amina—a seed of value, of beginning to understand her worth in Christ.

Amina's request gave me the opportunity to explain to her that her worth is not found in being a mother.

These are strange truths for a Muslim woman to process, and Amina struggled with it a bit. I could see that she did not understand the nature of sin. According to her faith, sin is only a weakness and is only serious if one is caught. Sins to her are categorized into big and insignificant. She had not done anything "big," like drink alcohol, eat pork or have premarital sex. And if she did sin she could simply be more diligent about saying prayers or fasting. Nevertheless, she did begin to process these new truths and was not resisting them.

It usually takes a number of tries before such biblical truths make sense to a Muslim. It takes time for strange, new words to percolate. And once they do make sense, the Muslim must have faith to believe them. It is important for us Christians to remember that we must depend on the Holy Spirit's anointing power in our witnessing, rather than on manuals, movies, entertainment or celebrities. We need to let Jesus shine in all His glory and majesty and let Him plant the seeds of truth in our friends' souls.

For now, at least, Amina had faith to believe that Jesus had healing power and could help her have a safe delivery. And as she found worth in becoming a mother, she was also beginning to process that her true and greatest worth was in being loved by God—a concept that would take a long time to fully understand.

And Jesus did answer Amina's prayer. One morning several months later my phone rang. It was Amina, whose fear of childbirth had risen considerably. She could not get hold of Omar. "Please see if you can phone him. I am going to have my baby," she said nervously. We were able to reach Omar, who raced home to take Amina to the hospital. A short time later the phone rang again. Amina had given birth to a healthy boy by C-section. She was elated to have been spared a normal delivery, considering it an answer to her prayer. She was at peace and bubbled over with joy, knowing her value as a woman had just risen in giving birth to a son. Since then Amina has given birth to many more sons. Today she presides over her large family like a beaming matriarch, and she enjoys an honorable reputation in her community.

Halima

Halima, a Somali Muslim woman, was not so fortunate. Finding worth in motherhood would prove to be challenging to her.

One night Halima called in great distress. A Muslim woman she knew had given birth at full term to her baby. Four hours later the mother bled to death. Halima, who was pregnant and due the next day, was frantic for comfort and reassurance. She feared for what might happen to her. I gave her all the comfort I could offer with kind words and prayer.

After two weeks I had not received news of Halima's delivery. I decided to call and see how she was doing.

"Oh, *Farahea*," Halima called me the Somali name for *Joy*, "something terrible happened to me." She began to cry. "My baby was born dead. And it was a boy. Allah is punishing me. I have bad luck." Halima was grieving deeply. She had not been permitted to attend the gravesite funeral, as only men were allowed to do so, according to their religion. She was trying to process her grief amidst almost unbearable personal shame, as if such a devastating blow were her fault.

> ***"My baby was born dead. And it was a boy. Allah is punishing me. I have bad luck."***

Quickly I drove to her house. Halima fell into my arms and sobbed. Her grief was unbearable, but her belief that she was being punished by Allah was even worse. My heart went out to this woman. Shut up in her apartment alone with her curtains closed, she was trying to make sense out of this death. She knew that some in her community were wondering what she did wrong, and she felt severe condemnation and abandonment. I cried with her. Our common humanity brought us together, and I truly grieved for her, loving her with all the love of Christ.

Taking my Somali Bible out of my purse, I said, "Halima, I know your grief is terrible. But do you know where your baby is? Your baby is safe in heaven with God, fully alive. The Bible contains beautiful words about heaven." She was surprised to see a Somali Bible, and I relayed to her how my mother had spent years translating it into Somali so that people like her could hear words of comfort from God. Then I had her read in her own language from the book of Revelation:

"I heard a loud shout from the throne, saying, 'Look, God's home is now among his people! He will live with them, and they will be his people. God himself will be with them. He will wipe every tear from their eyes, and there will be no more death or sorrow or crying or pain. All these things are gone forever'" (Revelation 21:3–4).

Halima looked confused. These were foreign concepts to her. God desires a home among His people? And heaven is called home? She sat there quietly letting the words of beauty and hope sink in. Then, looking up, she remarked dejectedly, "Well, we believe if our baby dies she will bring us fruit in hell." I could not believe it. She had by her own words destined herself to hell! Her only comfort was that her baby would bring her fruit. I knew it was not the time for me to give Halima a lesson on heaven and hell or to explain the differences between what the Qur'an and the Bible teach on these topics. She was in grief and pain. Further explanation would have to wait. I grieved with her and listened, loving her with the love of Christ. Before I left I asked if I could pray for her, which I did, and then I hugged her goodbye, promising to return soon.

I continued to grieve for Halima—for her loss of her baby, yes, but even more for her lost heart. Poor Halima. Her worth was not in who she was in Christ. She had placed all of her value in becoming a mother, and when her baby died it devalued her life completely. Her personal shame took her into self-condemnation and a long-lasting depression. I prayed she would learn of her true value as a beloved child of God.

Halima had placed all of her value in becoming a mother, and when her baby died it devalued her life completely.

Worldview and Worth

For many Muslim women, pregnancy and babies are rewards or signs of good luck. Barrenness and the death of a child, on the other hand, are bad luck and punishment. Their purpose in life revolves around producing children, which determines to a large degree how they feel about themselves, how their husbands or community reject or esteem them and how Allah views them. Again, it comes back to a worldview revolving around honor and shame.

In the Bible, Hannah was childless, and Peninnah scorned her, causing deep anguish for Hannah. Hannah responded to her cultural shame in the right way by going to God about it. But for the Muslim woman who does not know or understand the truths of the Bible, carrying shame for barrenness or losing a child is almost unbearable, and it often makes her a public spectacle of scorn. It is only through understanding and accepting how much God loves her that a Muslim woman can know her true worth. And every woman, regardless of her ethnicity or faith, needs to understand her true value and worth that is found only in Christ Jesus.

13

Revenge

I met Jasmin and her family shortly after they arrived in Canada as refugees from a war-torn country. A few of her family members had been executed by government agents, which seemed to be the case in many families. Jasmin's husband, Amir, had to disappear from their country quickly in order to stay alive. Overnight he lost his job, from which he had received respect and status, his house and his land. It was not only a desperate situation for Amir, but also one of public shame. Suddenly he and his family were without shelter and running for their lives. They spent a number of years in temporary housing in a neighboring Muslim country before they received permission to come to Canada.

Jasmin and Amir were Muslims, but they were not a practicing religious family. In truth, they were tired of having their lives ordered around by religious authorities who yelled at them, beat them and punished every act of straying from their harsh interpretation of Islam.

When I met her, Jasmin was like a wilted, droopy flower whose life and beauty had finished its day. Occasionally she would look at her hands, roughened by excessive hard work, and forlornly say to me, "Joy, I am getting old. And look at my face—my cheeks are sunken in." She did not want to look so tired and wilted, but she had no relief in sight. Jasmin made me think of the time our four-year-old granddaughter, Emily, observed some flowers in my backyard garden plot. "Grandma," she said sadly, "it looks like the flowers are trying to die." I was amused and consoled Emily that they were not trying to die but simply needed watering.

It was the same way with Jasmin. The "garden" needed watering.

Amir's Anger

We soon discovered that the wilted flower was about to surprise us with a resurrection. Jasmin had learned to be a survivor. Every day for years she had been a punching bag for her husband's uncontrollable blows of anger. Now living in the West with its inherent freedoms for women, Amir felt like he was losing power and authority over his wife. Suddenly he realized he had come to a country where women have rights that empower them—and not only women, but children, too! This frightened the very core of his male psyche, and his erratic, angry outbursts became more serious. While some men adjust quickly to our Western culture, even encouraging their wives to move forward, Amir could not. To keep Jasmin dependent upon him, he refused to let her learn how to drive, go to the bank or do any shopping. She was not allowed to call her family lest she report her struggles. Initially he did not allow Jasmin to go to English school for fear that she would prove to be smarter than he and get ahead quicker. Everything was spinning out of his control.

Nevertheless, Amir, apart from his violent anger episodes, was enjoyable to be around. He was intelligent and asked a lot of questions, especially about Christianity. Unlike many Muslims, he was not afraid to ask questions. We tried to understand his pent-up anger caused by the injustices he had endured in his country, his fear of Western culture weakening his power and identity as the man of the house and his shame at having to settle for a menial day security job.

Our families gathered frequently for meals in either their home or ours. It was fun exchanging recipes with Jasmin, who made an especially tasty delicacy from her country that she shared with me. Spending time in a kitchen together has a way of making women feel at home with one another.

"I saw my father kill family members," Amir said slowly, and then with great bitterness he added, "I was beaten twice with forty lashes for drinking a small amount of alcohol."

Jasmin also had a knack for decorating, and she transformed their low-income apartment into an attractive home. She was so delighted with decorated Christmas trees when she first saw them that she bought a secondhand tree and kept it up for months. She was just happy to finally be settled. Jasmin wanted to get on with life.

The more our friendship with Amir and Jasmin deepened, the easier it became to talk about the domestic abuse and Amir's escalating identity crisis as a man in the West. "Amir, you will need to learn new ways to deal with your anger now. It is against the law to beat your wife or children," my husband repeatedly instructed him. We could tell he was torn between a deep desire to change his ways and wanting to retain his perceived manly power of being in charge and having the right to do whatever he wanted. He did not want the added humiliation and shame of being viewed as a weak man.

"I saw my father kill family members," he said slowly, and then with great bitterness he added, "I was beaten twice with forty lashes for drinking a small amount of alcohol." I could tell he felt humiliated and shamed by that. Anger, mixed with shame and humiliation, often results in a strong desire for revenge.

Jasmin knew she could call the police for help, but she was scared to take such a bold step. But eventually it became a matter of survival, and she was forced to call them to be rescued from a beating. This proved to be a huge step of empowerment for her.

After that we often would witness Amir clutching his arms tightly, desperately trying not to raise them in a fit of anger. He knew he would be put in jail if he did not change his ways, and that scared him. Discovering her new empowerment, Jasmin suddenly realized she could stand up for her rights and freedoms, and for a while she misused them in order to punish or shame her husband. The new set of rights and freedoms for women initially confused both of them. It was like each was trying to gain the upper hand over the other.

I Will Never Forgive!

Our families began meeting together to study the Bible. It was a highlight of their week, as Amir and Jasmin became affected by the life and teaching of Jesus Christ. The more they learned about Him, the more they opened up to us, especially Amir. He, like many Muslim men, loved to write poetry, and he shared with us poems he had written about his mother—and about Jesus.

"We believe in Jesus," Amir repeated many times, but he meant that they believed what the Qur'an said about His being a prophet and performing miracles of healing. It is common to hear Muslims declare love for Jesus or say they believe in Him. They mean, however, that they love Him as a miracle worker or prophet, but not as Savior. Unless the Holy Spirit reveals their sin and they become convicted, they will not see any need of a Savior.

Amir and Jasmin loved and eagerly listened to the words of Jesus until we came to His stark words of instruction recorded in Matthew 5:43–44: "You have heard the law that says, 'Love your neighbor' and hate your enemy. But I say, love your enemies! Pray for those who persecute you!"

Exploding, Amir shouted, "I will never forgive my enemies. Never!" He began listing the terrible things his enemies had done—shameful things that to him were unforgivable. We had heard similar responses from more Muslims than we could count. Revenge can become an obsession. The thirst for revenge eats away at people, consuming minds and bodies.

> ***Exploding, Amir shouted, "I will never forgive my enemies. Never!"***

Well, we sat there in shock, not knowing what to do. We were speechless. Not able to navigate through the land mine that had just exploded, we softly began to sing "Jesus Loves Me." We sang it to them like a lullaby. It seemed a silly thing to do, but amazingly Amir settled down.

By the end of the evening we could see that those words of Jesus we had read from Matthew 5 were too demanding for Amir, and his desire for revenge closed down future Bible study times. Jasmin, on the other hand, chose to let go of revenge. She decided to live in the present and not let the injustices of the past fester and destroy her. Jasmin later confided in me, "Jesus has my heart, but my husband has my body."

Sharing Our Experiences

Amir's thirst for revenge reminded me of instances in my own life when bitterness and revenge consumed me. Several instances in particular stood out to me. Individuals had spread false rumors and written nasty letters about me. We had been robbed. Once a group of people attempted to kidnap my husband. These events were not easy to get over.

Often it is helpful to our Muslim friends when we share experiences from our own lives. Humbling ourselves, becoming transparent and vulnerable, divulging our weaknesses, struggles and wounds with them—these things reveal our common humanity and show that we Christians are not exempt from suffering. Far from acting worthy or superior, we need to come alongside fellow pilgrims and give them hope that Jesus can bring help, victory and transformation because we have found that to be true for ourselves. Especially when confronted with a Muslim's thirst for revenge, I share my personal experiences of bitterness and desire for revenge, and then I tell them about the forgiveness and freedom that is found in Christ.

"I have chosen not to keep a *hisab* ('account')," I share with my friends who also struggle with thoughts of revenge. I explain how the blood of Jesus helps me to forgive, and then I lead them in a practical demonstration. I write down my angry turmoil on paper. I mince no words in describing how I feel. Then I lift up the paper to Jesus, who understands our inner struggles, and I declare out loud, "Jesus, I choose to forgive him in the name of Jesus. I want to obey You, so I release forgiveness to him. I bless him in the name of Jesus, in the hearing of God the Father, the Son, the Holy Spirit and His angels and in the hearing of Satan and his demons. Help me, Lord!" My Muslim friends are usually shocked at my passionate anger. But when it comes to strongholds of revenge, we are in a war zone, and we are not dealing with a kitten. It is time to slay the dragon.

It is rare for people like Amir to be willing to let go of revenge and walk in the ways of Jesus. Revenge often is embedded into a person's culture from birth and is considered an honorable response to shame and humiliation. It can be passed from one generation to the next, even growing stronger with each generation. The desire for revenge and harboring bitterness, hate and fear—these are heavy burdens that can cripple people from moving ahead.

Earlier in my life my own burden was heavy, and it certainly crippled me. But God in His abundant mercy relieved me of the load I had carried since childhood. I had mastered how to cover up my internal fears, bitterness and desire for revenge, but I could not forgive my enemies. Then I encountered a surprise Visitor whose visit changed me forever.

When it comes to strongholds of revenge, we are in a war zone, and we are not dealing with a kitten. It is time to slay the dragon.

The Visitor came gently to my side one night as I lay dreaming. I dreamt I had a debilitating wound on my leg. It was infected with pus. A doctor in a white coat looked at it and remarked kindly in a concerned voice, "Joy, I will need to lance the wound to let the pus drain. There is a lot of pus in there."

Pulling back strongly, I replied, "No way. You cannot touch me." He tried coaxing me numerous times, but I would not budge. I was afraid He would hurt me.

The doctor would not give up. He knew the wound needed to be lanced, so we engaged in round after round of His coaxing and persuading and my resistance. Finally He looked tenderly at me and said, "I will be gentle with you. Just trust me."

At last I surrendered to His medical care. He lanced it gently, and I stared in utter amazement as pus began to ooze out, then grew and grew until it was a river flowing down the street.

"Oh, my goodness!" I exclaimed. "Where did all that come from?"

He replied kindly and gently, "I told you there was a lot. Now you will be okay." He cleansed the wound and bandaged up my leg.

I looked intently at Him for a long moment, and He smiled back in an understanding way. *He must be Jesus*, I thought.

When I awoke I pondered the graphic dream. Complete peace descended upon me. The moment was sweet and sacred. I felt whole. The poison of years of accumulated fears, bitterness and desire for revenge had taken its toll on me, but kind, gentle Jesus Christ, my beautiful Savior, came to my rescue and released the river of infection from within me, cleansing the wound and bandaging me up. There were no adequate words to say thank You.

Knowing the freedom in Christ that I felt that day, I can attest to its life-changing and life-giving power. Not only does Jesus offer us freedom from our anger, bitterness and desire for revenge, but He also offers us divine healing. Freedom and healing are the twin ministries of the Holy Spirit. I want all people, especially those of my Muslim friends who struggle with thoughts of revenge that are so much a part of who they are, to know that same freedom and healing. I have shared this encounter innumerable times with Muslims struggling with anger and desire for revenge, and it profoundly speaks to them. Sharing my experiences with them often helps to open their eyes to another way—the way of Christ.

Amir and Jasmin Today

We have grown fond of Amir and Jasmin, who have come a long way. Today Jasmin goes to the bank, shops, has a job and phones her family. She no longer looks like a wilted flower. It took time to revive her, but she is a wise woman who understands how to proceed in difficulties. I have learned from her wisdom. Jasmin is on a spiritual journey. When we share Christ with Muslims we are never quite sure at what point they decide to follow Him fully, as it is usually a long-term process involving years of processing new truths. But her declaration that "Amir has my body, but Jesus has my heart" indicated to me that she was well on her way into the Kingdom of heaven.

Behind Amir's anger and violence is a hurting person who has not been healed. If Amir would surrender his pain and injustices to Jesus, then he would find rest from his heavy burden. He has heard the words of Jesus in Matthew 11:28–30: "Then Jesus said, 'Come to me, all of you who are weary and carry heavy burdens, and I will give you rest. Take my yoke upon you. Let me teach you, because I am humble and gentle at heart, and you will find rest for your souls. For my yoke is easy to bear, and the burden I give you is light.'"

We continue to pray that, like Jasmin, Amir, too, will be able to say, "Jesus has my heart." We pray he will release the heavy burden he has carried for so long and find rest, freedom and healing in Jesus. Revenge, anger and violence are burdens too heavy for people to bear. They lead only to destruction. We must help our Muslim friends to know that Jesus is willing and able to take these burdens from them—if they will only let Him.

14

The Perfect Home

Yusef ran for his life. Government agents from his country searched for the fugitive, but Yusef managed to get across the border and find temporary shelter in another Arab country. He was exhausted and relieved to be out of imminent danger. His nightmarish memories of torture, however, were embedded in his memory. He could not forget his friend whose ear was cut off for not being loyal to the dictator. He could not forget his fellow prisoners who were taunted with mock preparation for hangings and forced to wear black hoods over their heads. He could not forget the brutal executions of his closest friends under the volatile regime.

Shortly after finding sanctuary in his temporary homeland, he was invited to a friend's home. He was impressed with the beauty and meekness of his friend's sister, Ayesha, who graciously and quietly served him a sumptuous meal. Soon Yusef and Ayesha married. A few years after their marriage they made their way to Canada, hoping for a bright future for their children. This was the beginning of this couple's search for a home.

Yusef's Anger

During their first few years in Canada, Yusef experienced a high level of agitation and frustration. Every time I visited he had a difficult time containing his anger toward the ruthless despot under whose rule he had lived. I wondered if he would ever put those days behind him. Without fail I would leave their apartment feeling as if I had stepped on a land mine. Land mines have a way of blowing us apart—if not physically, then emotionally. I was comforted by a dream I once had where Jesus coaxed me to take His hand to walk across a field of land mines. I absolutely refused. But He did not let up, and finally I surrendered and took His hand. We walked right across the field of land mines and came safely to the other side! I realized God was warning me that while doing His work among Muslims I would encounter many explosive land mines like Yusef, but I was to trust Him to bring me through them safely. I immediately notified my Emergency Prayer Community for backup support.

Part of Yusef's anger was expressed through religious zeal. At every visit he would express concern about my religious state. He would speak loudly and excitedly, making my blood pressure shoot up. Finally, not able to withhold his convictions any longer, he interrupted my English lesson with Ayesha and exploded vehemently, "Joy, you are going to hell! You do not wear a *hijab*. You will go to hell!"

Looking at him in shock, I answered quietly but firmly, "Actually, Jesus Christ will take me to heaven, Yusef." He kept at it until he finally realized he could not dominate the conversation and left Ayesha and me to our English lesson.

Yusef's Concerns

Yusef's anger was exacerbated by how uncomfortable he felt in our country, where women wear shorts and sleeveless tops and do not don the *hijab*. Modesty in dress is an especially sensitive matter to conservative Muslims. It is making a statement that the woman is upholding the honorable name of her family or husband by not appearing immoral or making herself available for inappropriate sexual advances.

Yusef began to be consumed with thoughts about where he should raise his daughters so they would not be led astray by the temptations and vices of the West.

Yusef was concerned about his daughters, whom he loved dearly and wanted to protect. He did not want Ayesha or his girls to become influenced by Western ways. I tried to be sensitive to his concerns and wear modest clothes to help him relax around me.

Yet Yusef began to be consumed with thoughts about where he should raise his daughters so they would not be led astray by the temptations and vices of the West. He missed home and talked endlessly about his country and family. Even while his daughters were preschoolers, he talked openly about moving back to his country or to some of the cities in Ontario where large Arab populations live. He wanted them to be safe living in a Muslim community where they could attend an Islamic school. He needed a safe Islamic environment to feel at peace.

Ayesha

Ayesha could not attend English school because she had many babies with hardly a break in between pregnancies, so she occupied herself at home by watching Arabic satellite television. This kept her from learning English quickly or assimilating into the new culture surrounding her. Physically she was in the West, but her mind and heart were in the East. She was often homesick for her family and longed to return to her country. I became intimately acquainted with the events in her family that were happening thousands of miles away: marriages, children, the latest engagement, difficulties of a newly divorced sister or the illness of her mother.

The satellite programs helped ease the awful loneliness tormenting her day after day. Often her ears were tuned into the Arabic satellite programs rather than on our conversation. Sometimes I just gave up trying to converse and watched them with her. I actually learned a lot about Lebanese, Yemeni and Sudanese cultures at those times! Occasionally the call to prayer would cry out from the satellite program. Hearing the familiar cry from the Muslim cleric over the loudspeaker coming right from her city back home made Ayesha feel more at home in her adopted land.

> ***Yusef needed a safe Islamic environment to feel at peace.***

Ayesha was a wonderful cook of Arab cuisine. She knew I was especially fond of stuffed grape leaves. Sometimes I sat on the floor making them with her. Doing it together, rather than just watching her, made us feel at home with each other. "You are doing great, Joy," she remarked, pleased that I was entering her world. She would spread out a plastic tablecloth on the living room floor and lay out numerous savory dishes. The family and we would sit around the tablecloth, picnic style, enjoying each other's company while a satellite Arabic program blared loudly in the background.

Ayesha obtained vegetable seeds from back home. Watching their little garden plot grow with vegetables unique to their country gave her and Yusef a lot of pleasure.

Where Is Home?

Both Yusef and Ayesha dreamed of the day when they would find the best place to raise their daughters. As they approached the day when they could officially apply for citizenship, feelings of loyalty to their homeland tugged at them relentlessly. Where is home after all? Where did they really belong?

> ***Both Yusef and Ayesha dreamed of the day when they would find the best place to raise their daughters.***

I understand that conflict well and can identify with their search and wandering. Perhaps that is one reason I feel at home among Muslims. Having been born in Yemen and having lived in Somalia, Ethiopia, Kenya, the United States, Pakistan, Canada and Tunisia in at least thirty different houses, I know that the search for a permanent home can gnaw relentlessly at people, making them feel like nomads on the earth. Living the life of a nomad is a rootless nightmare, one that is probably best observed among the Somali newcomers, who tend to move from city to city frequently. It is indeed a deep human pain for which there is no earthly remedy.

Immediately after the citizenship ceremony, Yusef, along with many other new citizens, raced to the government office to apply for the coveted Canadian passport. I recalled when I, too, joined other immigrants from around the world and became a dual citizen of the United States and Canada. The buzz of excitement and joy is palpable when that long anticipated day arrives. Yet for Yusef the joy was mitigated by homesickness for his country and concern for his family.

Moving

Yusef felt the tug to return home, so after taking a careful stock of his income he made a trip back to his country to check out the possibility of moving there permanently. He found, however, that the country still was not safe. He narrowly escaped a car bombing.

He returned to Canada and began to think more seriously about one of the more populated Arab cities of Ontario. Living there would bring them closer to Detroit, the Arab capital of North America. He and Ayesha were distressed by the discrimination they felt from their neighbors, and they became all the more determined to move somewhere else. They reasoned that living among their own people would make things better.

On a visit to them in early summer I was surprised to see their living room emptied of nearly all the furniture. "What's happened, Ayesha?" I asked.

"We are moving near Detroit," she stated. That was my last visit. The children were sad to leave, having to say goodbye to many friends. But Yusef and Ayesha were hanging on to the utopian hope that moving to a heavily populated Arab community within Canada would answer their need for a safe home where they would have freedom and could live among other Muslims.

Searching for That Earthly Home

After a decade of searching for an earthly home that would meet their expectations, Yusef and Ayesha still had not found their hearts' desires. I do not believe they will ever find the home their hearts are truly seeking. Why? Because that home can be found only in Christ Jesus.

As tensions and conflict arise in many Islamic nations, Muslims seek the freedom and safety that is found in the West. Yet the West often does not feel like home to them. It is important for us Christians to reach out to them, to help them feel more at home with us.

I do not believe they will ever find the home their hearts are truly seeking. Why? Because that home can be found only in Christ Jesus.

One of the most effective ways to reach out to them is to invite them into our homes. Hospitality touches them deeply, as it is a big part of their culture. And since they feel most comfortable in their own homes, they are delighted if we ask to visit them, too. They are honored.

But most of all it is important—and it is our commission—to listen to the leading of the Holy Spirit, who wants to use us to lead them to their one true Home. For only in knowing Jesus will they find the rest, peace and sense of belonging that fulfills their deepest need.

15

The Pull and Pressure of Community

As I learned from Yusef and Ayesha, Muslims moving to the West inevitably look to the one thing that is still familiar—community. It is of utmost importance to them. It is the glue that holds them together. Yet the wonderful sense of community found among Muslims can cause great confusion for Christians who are either accustomed to it or enticed by it. Even I myself have experienced this pull and confusion.

My Seduction

I was badly shaken and frightened to the core of my being. Sitting in my house, I stared at nothing in particular, frozen with an eerie feeling. A black cloud descended upon me, making my head feel like lead. A jumble of thoughts darted here and there. *If a person can drown in black thoughts,* I thought, *then this is it for me*. I was terrified because at that moment I was being seduced by the evil one.

I am really so much at home with Muslims, I thought, *and I feel so comfortable with them that I wonder what it would be like to actually be a part of them?* My imagination fast-tracked.

Warm memories flooded my mind. My Muslim friends were open and transparent, hospitable and always right there for me. When my husband had to go on a trip, I could count on them to keep me company. When I had my car accident, they were emotionally involved. When our son, Jonny, who was fifteen months old at the time, was run over by a van, it was Muslims who poured into our home before anyone else to show their care and concern. (Miraculously Jonny survived unharmed.) It was our Muslim friends who first offered us a place to stay when we were evacuated from our home during a flood. And whenever we had to move, our Muslim friends would be the first to offer their help.

I was terrified because at that moment I was being seduced by the evil one.

I remembered in particular dear Fazeela. After painstakingly caring for her small garden plot all summer and hoping for a good harvest of pumpkins, they all were stolen except one. In her sweet, sacrificial way she lovingly gave the lone pumpkin to me. It was such a kind gift that I wanted it to last forever.

I thought of the memorable evening when my North African friend invited me to her home. A group of North African women were there, most of whom I knew, including my friend's mother-in-law visiting from their village. She wore village attire, had tattoo markings on her face and had only one eye. The sweet, one-eyed matriarch was concerned about me because I did not look North African. She felt I was out of place and something had to be rearranged. My friend solved the problem by taking me into her bedroom and dressing me in her North African wedding outfit. I was transformed into a North African bride, complete with intricate henna designs on my hands. When I emerged from the bedroom, the women were overjoyed. The mother-in-law exclaimed in Arabic, "Allah! She is Muslim now."

"What did she say?"I asked my friend.

When she translated her mother-in-law's statement, I was horrified. I replied emphatically, "No, I am a Christian. These clothes do not make me a Muslim. But I like them a lot." I could tell, however, that all the women took me right into their hearts when I looked like one of them.

Muslims have shown me much kindness over the years. And of course, I loved the parties and festivities and spicy food. *I feel at home with Easterners,* I thought, *and Muslims in particular.*

Warm thoughts of Muslim community attracted me and pulled at me like a magnet. Suddenly the wooing came crashing down upon me, and I began to shake and feel weak. A silent sob rose deep within me, making me feel like I would choke. "Oh, Jesus, help me. I need You. Come, Lord Jesus. Help me!"

Inwardly I questioned, Lord, why did You give me such a deep love for Muslim women?

I thought of my wonderful Savior. I loved Jesus so much. He had done so many things for me over the years—miracles, healings, times of great protection, times of comfort, gifts of joy. I thought of His suffering on the cross for me. He had sacrificed His last drop of blood for me. I cried out, begging for help. Inwardly I questioned, *Lord, why did You give me such a deep love for Muslim women? I love them, and they love me in return—at least many of them do. They can be so loving and caring and sweet.*

I was being seduced and tempted and was in dire need of help and rescue. I wrestled inwardly until I cried out loud,

"Jesus, I will always stay true to You. I love You. I love You so much. I will enjoy and enter into Muslim community to share about You, but I will always choose You over community."

A sudden peace came over me. I realized that it was not the Islamic faith that was pulling at me. Rather, it was the magnetic pull of Eastern community.

I was a target of seduction by the evil one. If I had not been daily reading the Word of God and spending time in fellowship with Him through prayer, I believe I easily could have been devoured. But the Holy One who fights for us kept me secure. Jesus met me in my hour of need.

The way Jesus came to my immediate rescue reminded me of the many times I have witnessed how the one simple word *hooyo* ("mama") produces instantaneous response from a Somali mother. Her children may be roaming around a large store or park when through the air comes the piercing cry "*Hooyo*!" The whole world stops at that moment. *Hooyo*'s ears are highly attuned to her children's cries for help. Her inner radar instantly identifies her child and the direction from which his cry is coming. She flies off at lightning speed to meet the need, and soon all is well. Just like the Somali *hooyo*, in my hour of temptation and seduction the Holy Spirit came instantly to my plea for help and purified my allegiance to Jesus Christ. At the same time He was preparing me to come alongside two special sisters in Christ who would experience the magnetic, seductive pull and pressure of the Islamic community.

Rahima and Dunya

I met each of these two women about a week after their arrivals from their respective countries. Although the meetings were years apart, their stories are strikingly similar.

Both Rahima and Dunya had put their faith in Jesus before arriving in the West and came emotionally exhausted and deeply desirous of finding a safe environment in which to live out their new faith in Christ. It is not often that a Muslim woman takes the brave step of following Jesus Christ. Rahima had taken the even bolder step of being baptized. Such women are sometimes shunned in the Muslim community—or at least by family members. They lose their sense of familiar community and can feel like fish out of water. Rahima and Dunya had high hopes that coming to the free West would take care of the difficulties they had encountered as converts to Christianity. Yet they were strangers in a new land, and they felt lonely and unsure.

I observed their fight to stay part of their own familiar Muslim community while at the same time loving being with Christians.

When I welcomed them to my city, Rahima and Dunya both fell into my arms and clung to me for a long time. Our spirits bore witness together that we were one in Jesus. It was similar to that wonderful feeling when you walk through your front door after a long trip and a sweet contentment washes over you. You have finally arrived home. The moment I met Rahima and Dunya, God birthed in me a divine, sweet love for them. I could not recall having such deep love so quickly. I have sometimes pondered on the mystery and sweetness of it all.

Over the next months I spent precious hours with each of them studying the Bible, praying and singing worship songs. I watched both sisters navigate through adjusting to Western culture while tenaciously retaining a semblance of their own culture. They struggled with learning English and tried valiantly to assimilate into the Western Church. I observed their fight to stay part of their own familiar Muslim community while at the same time loving being with Christians. In time a network of caring Christians surrounded each of them. I interceded for them often, knowing that it would become only more difficult for them to stand strong as followers of Jesus.

The Going Gets Tough

When it came to Islamic religious festivities, weddings or funerals, both women understandably longed to be with their Muslim people groups and would enter into those events. At such times the wooing would begin. The pull of the Islamic community was inviting and welcoming for both of them. Tensions began to rise in both women. Their faces did not reflect as much peace. Before long both women became targets of fear tactics, although in completely different ways, and they felt more and more pressure to associate with the Islamic community. I will never forget the exact moment with both of them, each separately and many years apart, when I knew the journey for these sisters was becoming bumpy and confusing. The moment was clearly defined in each situation.

Both of these women have been buffeted while trying to stay true to Jesus. During some particularly brutal buffeting times, the magnetic pull, pressure and fear tactics have affected their minds. Praise the Lord, neither woman has denied Him. Yet they both have discovered that they are not as free in the West as they had expected to be. The laws for protection are here, but the pulls and pressures remain. A change in geography does not eliminate these.

Observing the trials Rahima and Dunya encountered, distress and anguish rose within me. I worried that they would not stand strong, and I continued to intercede for them. When the going got tough for Rahima, I occasionally would stand at my bedroom window that overlooks a peaceful pond and cry uncontrollably, begging God to strengthen her but also to strengthen me as I suffered intolerably observing her intense battles.

The Robe Dipped in Blood

One early Sunday morning I opened my Bible to Revelation 19:11–16 and read:

> Then I saw heaven opened, and a white horse was standing there. Its rider was named Faithful and True, for he judges fairly and wages a righteous war. His eyes were like flames of fire, and on his head were many crowns. A name was written on him that no one understood except himself. He wore a robe dipped in blood, and his title was the Word of God. The armies of heaven, dressed in the finest of pure white linen, followed him on white horses. From his mouth came a sharp sword to strike down the nations. He will rule them with an iron rod. He will release the fierce wrath of God, the Almighty, like juice flowing from a winepress. On his robe at his thigh was written this title: King of all kings and Lord of all lords.

"A robe dipped in blood." That meant the robe was red. What was the significance of that? I searched for the answer. The Holy Spirit was trying to get my attention, but I could not put the pieces together.

It was time for church, so we scurried off. Arriving, we found our usual place in the sanctuary. For weeks I had stared at the beautiful stained-glass window situated behind the pulpit. I had often sensed as I studied it that something was strikingly different about it, but I could not pinpoint what it was.

That morning, however, as I glanced at it, I gasped. "I got it! That's it! I got it!!" I whispered excitedly to Ed. In the beautiful glass picture Jesus is wearing a red robe, rather than the white one in which He is usually depicted. I could not recall seeing a picture of Jesus wearing a red robe before. The veil over my eyes suddenly opened to reveal another glorious glimpse of Jesus in a way I had not ever pictured him, and the meaning of the verses in Revelation fell into place.

I could not recall seeing a picture of Jesus wearing a red robe before.

The robe was red because it came from His own blood given sacrificially on the cross for all people, including me, my Muslim friends and even my enemies. And to crown it all, He wears a banner of victory and celebration on His robe declaring Him to be the Word of God, King of kings and Lord of lords. He is the true superpower of all superpowers! Jesus, with full authority by His shed blood on the cross and the empty grave, has defeated Satan and all his strategies, tricks, seductions, temptations and deceptions to destroy God's beautiful creatures—which included me and Dunya and Rahima. With that divine touch by the Holy Spirit, my strength was bolstered almost instantaneously. I had the immediate knowledge and comfort that the Holy Spirit was holding onto the souls of these sisters in Christ. Although they were vulnerable and I had no power to sustain them or keep them standing true, they were in the strong hands of Jesus. No one could snatch them from Him. He assured me that as much as I love them, He loves them far more!

Aliya

The pull of Muslim community is strong and attractive when one is inside it. The focus on people, the enjoyment of sharing food together, the warmth and affection expressed among each other and the immediate care extended to a person in need are striking drawing features. It is community that holds many Muslims together. It is what people miss the most if they choose to leave their Islamic faith and follow Jesus. If one chooses to leave Islam and its community, the amputation and the wooing and pressure to return can be overwhelming. It is sometimes so difficult that some even decide to keep the community but not necessarily the faith, just giving it lip service. Aliya was one example of this.

"I am not really a Muslim, Joy," Aliya stated matter-of-factly to me. "But I want to be with my people, so I pretend I am a Muslim." Many are like Aliya, booking their weekends with invitations to homes in the community for meals and socializing. If they are not going to someone else's place, then they are entertaining in their own homes.

One day I dropped by Aliya's and noticed she looked unusually tired. I asked her why.

"I get tired going out every Saturday night or having someone over to our place. I cannot find time to take care of the house and do my shopping," she lamented, adding, "but I have no choice. If we do not go, our friends will be offended, and then they will not come to our place." It sounded like a trap to me.

Aliya saw no option but to stay in the trap. She faced social expectations in order to remain in good standing in her community, and if she did not maintain that standing, then she would be alone in her new homeland. Her family was across the ocean. All she had that was familiar was her community. Western culture simply did not satisfy her. She could not imagine surviving without her community around her, even if she became exhausted from the expectations.

The Pull for Christians

Young Christian women, especially those of university age, can be drawn like a magnet to Muslim community.

Judy sat on my sofa, looking utterly weary. I listened to her sad story. Raised in a Christian home, she had once been involved in ministry, though that was difficult to imagine as she sat before me now. One day at work she had met a charming, handsome young Muslim man. He spoke respectfully to her and even mentioned needing to say his prayers. God was on his lips often. Eventually he invited her to his parents' home for an Eastern meal, which she was anxious to taste. His family was kind and warm, taking a sincere interest in her, and the food was delicious. The seductive pull of Eastern community found its way into her heart, and before she knew it the two were married. Judy had become disconnected from her Christian community and disillusioned because she did not get answers for her questions about Christianity, so she was vulnerable to seduction.

After fifteen years of marriage and three children, she woke up one morning feeling something was missing. It gnawed at her. She missed her community at church. She had not been allowed to go to church after they married, except for Christmas. Before she married Judy did not fully comprehend that once children came along her religious freedoms would be curbed and the children would be raised Muslim. She was a confused, sad woman—but mostly weary. Thousands of people in our country just like Judy are seduced every day by the close-knit Muslim community.

Community Will Fail

Yes, the strength of Muslim community magnetism can pull one in unaware. I have listened to many Muslims tell me, however, of the many ways their community has failed or dissatisfied them or has not been there in their time of need, or has even hurt them. Inevitably at some point any community will fail us. Community is not meant to be the fountain from which we drink to find our deepest satisfaction.

Indeed, Jesus is the One who will never fail us. Community may be taken away from us, fail us, dissatisfy us or hurt us, but Jesus will never do these things. We belong firmly to the One who has given His life for us, and our true home can be found only in Him as He makes His home in our lives. Only when our Muslim friends find this home can they find their true sense of belonging. Let us as Christians seek ever more to make Jesus our home, so that we can draw other people, including Muslims, to the One who will never fail them.

16

Goodbyes

"Joy, you need to come out of your room and eat something," Mom begged. I ignored her knocking at my bedroom door. Our departure from Ethiopia to the United States was creeping closer by the hour, and it was too painful for me. Refusing to accept reality, I had shut myself off in my bedroom. How could I leave behind the mountainous beauty of Addis Ababa, the lush, green hills of Kijabe and all my friends? How could I bear not ever sitting again with Fahima beside the charcoal fires?

My happy boarding school days in Ethiopia and Kenya were soon to become history. My school and friends were what brought me peace and joy. While separation from my parents nine months out of each year and living a thousand miles away from them had produced its fair share of insecurity and loneliness, boarding school was a safe, happy refuge for a timid, shy girl like me. At school I could sleep in peace, free from the fear of robberies or, worse yet, the possibility of murder. The thought of not being able to finish my final year of high school at the academy brought both tears and anger. *It is just not fair*, I inwardly seethed.

Months earlier, Dad had taken my twin brother, John, and me on one final trip to visit the towns of Beled Weyne, Bulo Burti and Baidoa in Somalia. I had not realized at the time that I was saying goodbye to the land and people of my childhood. It had not always been safe, but nevertheless, it was home. Never again, I lamented, would I see the proud-looking camels, heads held high as they crossed the hot desert landscape, or see the towering anthills that were such familiar sights in the interior of Somalia.

I picked up Pussy Wussy and cradled her in my arms one last time. While I stroked her fur, hot tears stung my eyes. Everything was suddenly being snatched away from me. When I bade final farewell to my childhood home a day later, I felt like my heart would break.

I never have revisited my childhood home in Mogadishu, Somalia. But in my mind's eye I can picture clearly the tall office, school building and house behind the theater on Sheikh Sufi Road. I remember as a teenager when romantic desires began to awaken in me and I would stand in the cool of the evenings at the railing overlooking the theater, dreaming about being held in the arms of a lover.

It is hard to imagine romance and weddings taking place in that city today. It has gone through so much destruction and bloodshed in the past few decades. Countless thousands of Somalis have fled my childhood city since I lived there, leaving their beloved homeland behind and not knowing if they will ever step foot in it again. Often they have had to say painful goodbyes in fleeing, rushed moments, not even having time to collect cherished photos or mementos to take with them.

Goodbyes are indeed painful and hard to accept, but especially so for the Muslim, who has little certainty or comfort in what is to come.

The Separation of Death

Final goodbyes in times of death are incredibly difficult for Muslims to face. Numerous Muslim friends have responded to news of death's finality with great fear and discomfort.

"Do not tell Manal that her sister died, Joy," Manal's husband called to tell me. He was trying to prepare the way for the news to be broken to his wife. "She is planning to call you soon to see if you know what has happened. Just tell Manal that her sister is sick."

When I asked a Bengali friend if she drove, she confessed with a degree of embarrassment, "No, Joy, I have not learned to drive because I have to pass a cemetery near my house, and I always close my eyes when I pass by it." I agreed that would be a problem while driving, and I tried to discuss the subject of death with her but to little avail.

Fadwa bought a book to learn how to speak with a departed person. She knew this practice was forbidden in Islam, but she missed her mother so badly and longed to hear her voice. She followed the instructions and began speaking with what she believed was her mother's spirit, but she never received peace or comfort. When I met Fadwa she had been doing these séances for years, and the activity had become an addiction from which she wanted to break free.

Shaheen, who was still recovering from surgery three months earlier, had good reason for her anger. "I am so angry, Joy, because for three months I was calling back home to see how my mom was doing. My brother always told me that she was out. It did not make sense. I was not able to sleep well for three months, worried that something was wrong with my mom. Now the family finally told me that Mom died three months ago."

Two years after she became a widow, Khadija sadly shared with me, "I have not moved any of Mohammed's clothes or books or aftershave out of their places since he died."

Afia had to make two trips to her homeland nearly back to back in order to attend funerals for both her mother and father. No one and nothing could console the grief in her soul—not even a new house worth half a million dollars. She showed off her granite countertops and backsplash in her new kitchen, then sitting down she cried out, "Joy, it does not feel like home. It does not make me happy."

I sat beside Salima as she dialed the phone number for her family back in her homeland. A message had been left on her answering machine that her father had died halfway around the world. Her husband had just left the day before to visit his family overseas and would be gone a few months. She was left alone. As a family member answered her call, Salima began wailing inconsolably and hysterically over the phone, rocking back and forth and wiping her teary face with her large, cotton headscarf. I have heard that kind of heart-wrenching wailing many times, and it sends shivers down my spine every time. I put my arm around her while she wailed over and over again.

Death is most frightening to Muslims who have no assurance as to where they will spend eternity.

Saying final goodbyes to loved ones is lonely and painful for all people. But death is most frightening to Muslims, who have no assurance as to where they will spend eternity. They can only hope in God's mercy.

Nasrin's Dream

Nasrin's brother had been sick, and she was deeply distressed the day the doctors gave her the grim news that there was no more hope for him. She went home and decided she would not pray anymore since her prayers had not been answered. Then she had a dream.

On one side of the road Nasrin saw destruction from an earthquake and ruined buildings. On the other side she saw big, beautiful villas. Between two of those villas, which were colorfully lighted, was an empty piece of land. A voice informed her that land was for her home. At first she was upset that one of the completed villas was not for her, but when she looked back to the other side of the road with ruined homes, she thanked God for giving her a place on the better side of the road. A voice called her by name and said, "Nasrin, this place is for your home, but it is not the time for you. Go back and prepare it. You will come back later."

Nasrin shared this dream with me one evening after eating supper in our home. I assured her the dream was God speaking to her about the eternal home He wanted to prepare for her in heaven. I told her that God had not finished preparing the home because she was not yet ready for it.

"What do you mean, Joy?" she asked, eager for an explanation. I got my Bible and, as I have done with many of my Muslim friends, read Jesus' words to His disciples in John 14:1–3:

> Don't let your hearts be troubled. Trust in God, and trust also in me. There is more than enough room in my Father's home. If this were not so, would I have told you that I am going to prepare a place for you? When everything is ready, I will come and get you, so that you will always be with me where I am.

"Nasrin," I explained, "God wants to prepare an eternal permanent home in heaven for you, but first your name must be registered in the Book of Life."

"What do you mean, Joy?"

I opened the Bible again and read Revelation 20:11–15:

> And I [John] saw a great white throne and the one sitting on it. The earth and sky fled from his presence, but they found no place to hide. I saw the dead, both great and small, standing before God's throne. And the books were opened, including the Book of Life. And the dead were judged according to what they had done, as recorded in the books. The sea gave up its dead, and death and the grave gave up their dead. And all were judged according to their deeds. Then death and the grave were thrown into the lake of fire. This lake of fire is the second death. And anyone whose name was not found recorded in the Book of Life was thrown into the lake of fire.

"After hearing and understanding the story of Jesus according to the Bible," I explained, "you have an opportunity to choose whether you accept Jesus as your Savior and Lord or not. If you choose to put your faith in Him, then your name will be registered in the Book of Life. You know that nobody is born a Christian, even if your mother and father are Christians."

Like every Muslim woman to whom I explain this biblical concept, Nasrin was confused. "You weren't born a Christian?" she asked. "What do you mean? Weren't your parents Christians?"

"No, my friend, no one can be born a Christian. It is impossible. You say you are born Muslim. But we cannot be born Christian, even if our parents are Christians. We become a Christian only when we understand who Jesus is and decide for ourselves to follow Him the rest of our lives. That is when our names are registered in the Book of Life—not at our physical birth. I was born into a family where my mother and father were Christians. I was born as a child of godly missionaries, but I was ten years old when I became a child of God through Jesus Christ."

I have explained this many times to Muslim women like Nasrin, Salima, Fadwa and Manal who have been faced with the deaths of loved ones and fearful of their own destinies. I have prayed for many that they would accept the truth and that their names would be registered in the Book of Life.

Mom's Grand Entrance into Heaven

When my mother died, my Muslim friends responded to the news with mixed feelings. They wanted to show sympathy and empathy and were curious about the details surrounding her death, but most of them were afraid to discuss the subject in any depth because the concept of death is terrifying for them. Yet I love to tell them the story of her entrance into heaven because it is such a beautiful testimony to the gift of eternal life through the Lord Jesus.

My mom was really peaceful when she started to exit this world. One day as she lay in her reclining chair she asked me, "Are there any messages you want me to take?" I was taken back a bit by her directness.

"Yes, you can tell Bashir that I visit Nafiza, his widow," I replied, trying to navigate my way into her foggy world.

"Any other messages?" she persisted. She knew her time was almost here, but she knew no fear, for to her, death was a grand entrance into the presence of Jesus, whom she loved deeply. She had spent much of her life doing God's work, translating the Bible into the Somali language so that Somalis would be able to read the full story of Jesus Christ in their own language. Now her Lord was soon to welcome her to her final, permanent Home. A view of the three crosses on Calvary's hill lit up the television screen in the room as we chatted.

"Mom, you are going to see Jesus soon."

"Yep!" she mustered enthusiastically. For her, heaven was all about seeing Jesus—and Aunt Martha, and my brother Charlie, and Adan, who had assisted her in the Bible translation, and so many others who had already gone to be with Him.

I had to leave her bedside in Florida to return to Canada to care for my family's needs. *Please, Lord, would You be so kind as to let me know when my mother is at death's door so I may speak with her one last time?* I pleaded with God.

A couple of weeks later in the middle of the afternoon after returning from the mall, I sat on the edge of my bed and began crying. "Why am I crying?" I asked myself, bewildered and trying to identify what caused the sudden flow of tears. Then I knew instinctively that I should call Mom. Dad answered the phone and in a somber, flat voice said, "Joy, Mother has been in a coma for three days. She is about to go. You will not be able to talk to her."

But I persisted, believing that God wanted to answer my request. "Just put the phone next to her ear," I urged Dad. When he did, I said, "Hi, Mom."

She answered back in a strong voice, "Goodbye, darling, I love you!"

In a few hours she made her grand entrance into the presence of Jesus in heaven. Home with Jesus! Imagine! I was overcome with grief but filled with wonder that God had given me such a kind gift.

Their faces reflect a longing and yearning to know for certain if heaven could be their eternal home.

My Muslim friends never tire of hearing this account. Their faces reflect a longing and yearning to know for certain if heaven could be their eternal home. My level of feeling more at home with them increases substantially at these moments. They are coming closer to understanding, and it is thrilling beyond description.

Dad's Departure from This World

Dad's departure from this world was surreal, too. I love to tell my Muslim friends about his death.

Not long before he died I became convinced inwardly that he was soon going to leave this world, and I persuaded our married daughter, her husband and our son to make the trip to visit Grandpa. We booked a one-week charter flight to Florida. A healthy and vigorous 91 years old, Dad did not look like he was near death's door at all.

One night he helped our daughter make a big batch of fresh orange juice. The next morning at breakfast time, I went to the bedroom to call Dad to the table, thinking he would be looking forward to the juice. He was fully dressed, shoes on, and lying on the bed with his hand on his open Bible. I nudged him, telling him that breakfast was ready. No response. I tried again. He was still warm to the touch. I knew his soul had flown off to heaven, and it had been a peaceful departure.

Dad had always told us he was going to die with his shoes on. And he died just like he wanted—busy right to the end. My daddy, whom I had been so terrified would be killed by a dagger, died peacefully reading his Bible at a ripe old age. Now he was home with Jesus—and with Mom, and with the precious Somalis who had given allegiance to Jesus and then given their own lives to stay true to their Savior. Saying goodbye to Dad—and to Mom—was painful, but it was not final. We will meet again in our eternal, heavenly Home. What a joyful reunion that will be!

"Your father was a good man," my Muslim friends tell me when I share this story with them. "That is why he died like that with no suffering."

"No, my friends. It was not because he was a good man. My mother suffered a lot before she died, and she had been a good woman." Numerous assumptions of peoples' deaths being either a punishment or reward are often discussed.

My daddy, whom I had been so terrified would be killed by a dagger, died peacefully reading his Bible at a ripe old age.

Upon my return from his funeral in Florida, the phone began ringing.

"I am so sorry, Joy, to hear your news," my Muslim friends phoned consolingly.

Keeping up my scheduled appointments to their homes, I sat on living room floors eating the meals they had lovingly prepared to show me their sympathy. My Muslim friends comforted me. They did not send beautiful bouquets of flowers, but they offered me a sweet sense of comfort as I sat beside them, often in long moments of empathetic quietness. *They certainly know how to show sympathy*, I thought, *even if they do not have a sure hope for the next life*. I received only one card from my Muslim friends, as sending cards is not really a part of their tradition. It was homemade, not from a store. Intisar had lovingly decorated it with a cross made out of shiny gold paper and had written simply, "Dear Joy, please accept my sympathy for your father's ?! I love you, and I always pray for you and your father and mother in heaven. Your friend, Intisar." For my friend Intisar, the word *death* was so terrifying that she could not even write it on her homemade card.

Sharing about Heaven with Muslims

Eventually we all have to say goodbye to members of our earthly communities. People die, leave us, deprive us of their presence, disappoint or hurt us. But there are no final goodbyes when Jesus has made His home in our hearts, not even at the moment we breathe our last breath on this earth.

When I bring up the subject of heaven with my Muslim friends, without fail they evidence a keen longing and desire to know more. The Qur'an speaks of heaven, though its descriptions are quite different from the biblical heaven. The Qur'an offers many references to a terrifying hell, and my Muslim friends live in dread and fear of going there. My Muslim friends fear death because their eternal destiny is unknown, although they hope their good deeds will outweigh their bad deeds and that in the end Allah will have mercy on them. There is no sure hope for Muslims. "Allah is merciful," they each affirm strongly. But inside they are not sure.

The Bible gives us beautiful information about heaven. It also speaks of hell and its torments. What a tremendous consolation and sure hope we have that Jesus is fully able to bring us to heaven and spare us from hell when we put our trust in Him. Reading these Scriptures to Muslims and teaching them these truths opens up a whole new world for them. They have not heard or been able to understand the Good News that Jesus, the Authority and Keeper of the keys of heaven and hell, has made it possible to be spared from hell and granted a sure entrance and welcome to heaven.

17

At Home with Sisters

I feel at home with Muslims. I feel most at home, however, when I am with my sisters in Jesus. They are like family, and we belong to each other.

Hanan and Her Dolls

I dropped by the home of my friend Hanan, of whom I am quite fond, to wish her a happy birthday. Hanan ushered me into her bedroom so we could chat. Usually we talked in the living room or went out to eat, so I was especially honored to be taken into her world and knew this signified a higher level of feeling at home with one another.

Hanan showed me the jewelry and precious trinkets on her dresser and explained how she loved playing her guitar that was propped on its stand in a corner of the bedroom. Opening her closet door, she said, "Joy, I want to show you some of the birthday gifts I received when I was a child." She reached for boxes on the top shelf and brought them down to show me three beautiful dolls in original packaging that still looked new.

Feeling somewhat confused as to why these childhood gifts were hidden on a top shelf in her clothes closet, I asked, "Hanan, have you never played with the dolls?"

"No, Joy, I was told they were so beautiful that if I played with them they might break, and so I never have taken them out of their packages. Aren't they beautiful, Joy?" she exclaimed, obviously still delighted with them.

"Well, yes, Hanan, they are beautiful, but dolls are meant to be played with. This way you never have been able to enjoy them." But Hanan was satisfied with the gifts of the dolls, even if they had been stored away unopened for years.

It made me think of how some Christians treat the amazing gift of salvation. They know exactly when they received the gift of eternal life and salvation, but they have never opened up and enjoyed the best gift the world has ever known—God, who came to us in human flesh as Jesus Christ.

Muslims who have not yet received the gift of salvation are like children opening a special gift and reveling in the thrill of what they have received.

I tried to explain this analogy to Hanan. She looked puzzled and asked, "Joy, how do you enjoy the gift of salvation?" So we began to open up the gift. As we did, a look of complete surprise overtook Hanan's face. This was something new to her. Enjoy Jesus? Believe in Him, yes, but enjoy Him?

"Yes, Hanan," I shared passionately with her. "God did not mean for us simply to receive the gift of salvation; He intends for us to enjoy our Savior."

Indeed, salvation is a gift God means for us to enjoy. Muslims who have not yet received the gift are like children opening a special gift and reveling in the thrill of what they have received. While Muslim women unanimously declare they believe in God, or Allah, as they refer to Him, it is only when the veil is removed from their spiritual eyes and they see God in all His glory in the person of Jesus Christ that they realize the magnitude of this divine, glorious gift and begin to enjoy its splendor.

Farzana's Gift of Salvation

When Farzana speaks of Jesus it is obvious she enjoys her gift of salvation. Her black eyes sparkle and shine, and often tears stream down her face because she cannot get over the wonder of Jesus' love for her. I love to hear her say the name *Jesus*. She speaks reverently and in awe of Him. Farzana has opened the gift of Jesus, her Savior.

To Farzana the gift of Jesus defines love—something she did not know growing up. Her home life was dismal. Constant fighting, cursing and cruelty were daily realities. Her paralyzed father was bedridden for most of her childhood, leaving her desperate mother to care for many young children alone. Farzana's mother beat her often. Hussein, a male relative, was especially cruel, and she lived in fear of him. One time he boxed Farzana's sister's ear so hard that she lost her hearing. When Farzana was eight years old she wanted to visit her grandmother and went skipping over to her house. Hussein came after her in a rage and with his big hand clawed her face, leaving it bleeding and scarred to this day.

Farzana wanted to run away but had nowhere to go. Home was not a safe refuge for this girl. Little love was shown or expressed in this family. No one talked much to each other. If anything was said it was negative. No one except for Hussein had the freedom to go to someone's house or even to pick up the phone. Others were not allowed to visit Farzana's home either. It was like a prison. The family went through the religious rituals of fasting and saying prescribed prayers, but that did not bring any joy or peace into the home. During Ramadan, Farzana's mother abstained from smoking, which is obligatory, but she went crazy without her cigarettes, and the cursing and swearing stepped up considerably, causing Farzana great agony.

Every decision was under the tight control of Hussein and Farzana's mother, including whom the children should marry. Farzana's sister fell in love with a young man, and they desperately wanted to marry but knew doing so would incur the family's wrath. When her mother discovered their relationship, she took Farzana's sister into the basement and beat her with a big rod, leaving her emotionally and physically wounded. Farzana shook with fear that her turn would soon come. Desperate to escape the hell at home, Farzana's sister managed to break out of the fortress and ran away and married the young man.

When Farzana met her future husband she discovered he was a Christian and knew immediately that would be a serious problem for her family. He gave her a book explaining Christianity. She heard for the first time that Jesus is more than a prophet. As was expected, her mother was not happy about the news and wiped her hands of responsibility. They had a small wedding.

Farzana's husband introduced her to his Christian friends at church. She was moved by their love and kindness and testimonies of what Jesus had done for them. Farzana was deeply affected by Jesus' words in John 14:6: "I am the way, the truth, and the life. No one can come to the Father except through me." One momentous day she stood up in front of them all and declared, "I want to give my life to Jesus." She had become convinced that Jesus is God and her Savior, not just a prophet, and this is no easy decision for a Muslim woman to make.

A few years later Farzana and her husband left their homeland and made their way to a neighboring country. Their shelter on the first night in their new country of refuge was in a park exposed to the elements of nature. Over the next few years they witnessed numerous miracles from God, particularly in the area of providing for their daily needs in a destitute situation. God's miracles of provision strengthened her faith tremendously.

From the beginning of meeting my sister Farzana I felt right at home with her. Our spirits are united in Jesus. The humility and love of Jesus captivates her soul in adoration.

The story of Jesus' cruel death on the cross is precious to Farzana. When she reflects upon the cross, tears fill her eyes, and she looks upward and whispers "thank You" to Jesus. We were chatting one day when Farzana exclaimed, "Joy, just think—Jesus paid the price for the punishment of my sins!" Farzana has known her fair share of punishment for every kind of infraction, and she can hardly believe that Jesus took the punishment she deserves upon Himself. She revels in this love of Jesus. Nearly every time we pray together she prays for family back in their homeland, who still live in spiritual darkness. She is amazed at the love and forgiveness in her heart for them and knows that comes only from Jesus' power.

Iman and the Internet

I also feel at home with Iman, who is from North Africa, because we are united in spirit and have become sisters. You see, Iman, too, has opened the gift of Jesus, her Savior.

Iman comes from a moderate Muslim family that keeps the month of fasting and says the prayers, but the women do not wear the *hijab*. Apart from losing her mother at six years old, Iman had a happy childhood living in a North African city near a beautiful beach. When she was eight she attended school at a vacated Roman Catholic church, which had previously been occupied by expatriates who had left the country. Iman remembers staring at the windows painted with beautiful pictures of Mary and Jesus, but she did not know who they were. The images have remained in her memory to this day.

Iman later studied accounting and then married Mohammed after a friend arranged for them to meet. Mohammed was a religious man who said his prayers faithfully and wanted Iman to wear the *hijab* once they had children. Mohammed wanted the children to know without a doubt that their mother was a good Muslim, and wearing the *hijab* communicated this to him. For the time being he allowed Iman to go without the *hijab*, but he did not let her wear makeup, fingernail polish, sleeveless clothes or tight pants because he considered these to be what immoral "Christian" women wear, as exemplified in Hollywood movies.

Mohammed suddenly announced that he had become a follower of Jesus!

After three years of marriage Iman and Mohammed made their way to the United States, where their children were born. But instead of enforcing Iman to wear the *hijab*, as they had agreed, Mohammed suddenly announced that he had become a follower of Jesus! This was alarming and astonishing news for Iman. Fighting broke out, and she threatened to call his family. While Iman herself was not particularly religious or even very knowledgeable about Islam, being a Muslim was her identity from birth, and her whole family was Muslim. She believed Islam was the last religion. She had heard that the Bible had been changed and that Jesus was only a prophet.

Mohammed urged Iman to explore Christianity. At the same time they discovered that Mohammed had developed a large tumor, which required surgery. Iman believed this was Allah's punishment for Mohammed's leaving Islam. But when the surgery cleared up anything serious, her superstition that it was a punishment was laid to rest.

"How did you discover what Christianity is all about?" I asked Iman one day.

"Well," she reminisced, "Mohammed explained a lot of things to me, but he also suggested that I check out a website called paltalk.com, where I could choose a nickname and enter a chat room anonymously. I chose a chat room in which Christian Arabs discussed Islam and Christianity in Arabic. I just listened to the discussions for a long time. After that I asked Mohammed a lot of questions, such as why God became a man."

"What happened then?" I pressed Iman, curious to know the whole process of her coming to understand the truth of Jesus Christ.

"After I listened to paltalk.com for a long time and after Mohammed had answered many of my questions, I left Islam but did not have any faith for about six months. Then Mohammed urged me to read the *Injil* ('the gospels') in Arabic. But even though I was educated in Arabic, I was not able to read the *Injil* at all, no matter how hard I tried. The ability to read the words was blocked."

"Do you understand why, Iman?" I inquired.

"Today I do. I realize that Satan did not want me to read it and prevented me from doing so, but back then I did not know what was going on," she explained.

"Then what happened?"

"Mohammed told me that if I could not read I could at least use my ears to listen. So he told me to go to a website called haya.org, which has a lot of Arabic Christian sermons and songs on it. I chose to listen to the gospel of Matthew being read in Arabic. I was really affected by Jesus' teaching in Matthew 5–7. It was His teaching that convinced me. Mohammed also asked me if I knew where I would go after I died. I knew there was not any answer to that question in the Qur'an. But I found the answer in Jesus' teaching. I became convinced He was more than a prophet. When I accepted Jesus as my Savior I received eternal life and forgiveness of my sins. But most of all I discovered that I could have a relationship with God because of Jesus—something that Islam could not offer me."

Iman received and opened the gift of Jesus and spends her life directing Muslims to also discover the gift of salvation. She wants to share this gift with others and not put it on a shelf, hidden away and left only as something received four years ago. It is a delightful joy that knows no bounds when sisters like Iman and Farzana and I can pray together. We are at home in the Kingdom! They are discovering there is a much bigger community of sisters and brothers beyond themselves.

Since she has received and opened the gift of Jesus, Iman wants to share this gift with others and not put it on a shelf, hiding it away. She now spends her life helping other Muslims to discover the gift of salvation. Because she came to know the truth of Jesus Christ through the Internet, she understands the need of many Muslims to receive a presentation of the Gospel in their own homes, away from public monitoring, which could get them into trouble. Today Iman is involved in an Arabic evangelistic Internet ministry here in the West and ministers to her own people across the ocean in North Africa and the Middle East. I am honored to call her my sister and fellow worker in the Kingdom.

Sabrina's Vision

Sabrina comes from the same kind of family that Iman does. Both families are more cultural Muslims than religious. Growing up in North Africa, Sabrina knew that her mother, in times of distress or need, often visited a Muslim man they considered a "saint." This practice is common in North Africa, and such "saints" are believed to have miracle-working powers.

Sabrina's childhood in North Africa was full of sadness. Her parents verbally fought each other regularly, and Sabrina's father was absent a lot of the time, leaving her mother frustrated with much parental responsibility. In addition, for generations Sabrina's family had harbored bitterness and unforgiveness. If someone hurt her family, they would immediately cut off all relationship with that person forever. They offered no room for forgiveness and would brood with bitterness, revenge and endless cycles of negative thoughts. Sabrina struggled with the same kinds of negative and revengeful thoughts that her mother and grandmother had. She wanted to be purified from these powerful thought patterns but could not seem to find freedom from them.

After Sabrina immigrated to the West, she was befriended by a Christian woman from the country of Benin who worked at the immigration settlement center. Sabrina asked her for a Bible. She had many questions, and the Muslims' prophet, Mohammed, had taught that Muslims should read the previous holy books to find answers. She began attending church with her new friend and attended an *Alpha* course (a study course started by a church in England that reaches out to seekers of all faiths and provides a forum for them to ask the difficult questions), but she still continued to struggle in particular with the concept of the Trinity.

Then God spoke to Sabrina through a vision. She saw Jesus in a white robe with gold and green trim. His face was shining, and He was coming toward earth. He spoke to her concerning her struggle to believe in the Trinity, and after pondering His words for two weeks, she became convinced that He was her Savior and surrendered her life to Him. Alone in a room, she declared, "I recognize, Jesus, that You are Lord." At that moment she felt a gentle wind sweep over her face.

A month later Sabrina shared the joy of her dream and decision with her friend and then her pastor. A few months later she was baptized. Today Sabrina is growing in the knowledge of the Word of God and is opening the gift of salvation. She is finding freedom from the torturous bondage of negative and revengeful thoughts toward people who hurt her. Through her Lord Jesus, she has found power to forgive them and no longer cuts off relationships with people who hurt her.

Rania No Longer Has to Measure Up

Unlike Iman and Sabrina, Rania was raised in a strict, religious Muslim family in Southeast Asia. Her entire childhood was dominated by Islamic culture and customs, which regulated every part of her life. It was of paramount importance to her family to obey all the laws of Allah. Rania, therefore, acquired more and more knowledge of the Qur'an, receiving top marks during her twelve years of private schooling that took her deeper into both the academic and theological study of Islam. Later she taught the Qur'an to children and youth. She began to view life as a battle—a personal, spiritual battle that must be won. Her focus was on pleasing Allah and getting approval from him and other people. But by the end of each day she felt frustrated and guilty because she was never assured that she could measure up to Allah's standards or please everyone else. Even on those rare days when she felt she had won this battle, she still felt something was missing.

Rania's desire to please Allah was not motivated by the affections of her heart, but rather by a deep-seated fear of being punished by Allah and suffering in hell. Death, therefore, was especially feared because it meant the start of terrible suffering.

Indeed Rania experienced many fears as a Muslim. Every night before going to sleep she would recite verses from the Qur'an, blowing them into the four corners of her room, believing that doing so ensured her protection from any possible harm from Satan. She placed a Qur'an on a shelf in her room as an added means of protection. Her family, like many Muslim families, lived in fear of people doing sorcery or placing curses on them. From early childhood she was afraid of bad *jinn*, which are believed by Muslims to be evil supernatural beings made out of fire. She had a strong belief in the *Dajjal*, an individual somewhat similar to the Antichrist of the Bible who is identified by Muslims as having only one eye and being able to seduce and deceive people with miracles in the end times. This belief drove her to stay as close to Allah as possible. She did not want to be deceived by the *Dajjal* if he should appear in her lifetime. She believed that the more she recited her prescribed prayers, the more she would be protected from the harm of the *Dajjal*.

Before Rania came to the West she taught English in a school in her country, where she was dedicated to her two hundred pupils and felt esteemed. After arriving in the West she desired to improve her English, so she began attending a church and became involved in a small Bible study group with the hope that doing so would improve her English. She also hoped to find a group where she could develop friendships.

Rania was quickly moved by the love, joy and acceptance she felt from these Christians. These were things she had not experienced in her Muslim community. Furthermore, Rania began to find a sense of comfort reading the Bible that she had not found reading the Qur'an.

But it was difficult for Rania to accept that Jesus is God and that He died on the cross and came back to life after being dead in the grave for three days. The concept of being made righteous, or pure, by Jesus' sacrifice instead of her own efforts was too good to be true for her. As a religious Muslim, Rania believed that everything is earned by hard work. She also had been taught from childhood that the Bible had been changed. Rania read Lee Strobel's books *The Case for Christ* and *The Case for Easter*, and these helped to convince her that the Bible is historically reliable and that the lie she had been taught was just that—a lie. Even though the Holy Spirit was showing Rania all the proof she needed to commit her life to following Jesus, she still needed more confirmation. She became desperate and begged God either to reveal His identity to her or to let her die because she could not live in confusion any longer. God soon gave her that confirmation. Following are Rania's words describing the encounter:

"I met Jesus in a dream. He was wearing a light-colored robe and was up high, looking down at me. His face was too bright to look at. I dared Him to prove if He was truly God and told Him that if He did, I would give my life to Him," she relayed, obviously full of emotion as she relived the vivid memory of her dream.

"After I dared Jesus in my dream to prove He was God and not just a prophet, I found myself struggling to breathe and became scared that I would suffocate to death. I felt my life becoming disconnected from me. But then I saw Him sitting beside me. He touched my forehead, and I was able to breathe again. I was convinced that His claim to be God was true. But then I doubted again, thinking that this was just another dream or the result of concentrating my thoughts on Him.

But the same scary process repeated again, confirming to me that this was not just a dream. Feeling I had been given a chance to live again, I recognized Jesus as my Savior and Lord. Before the dream was over Jesus said to me, 'What I said to you is not from Myself, but from My Father.' Later I discovered those words are similar to words recorded in the gospels. With the extra confirmation of those words and this dream, I finally put my faith in Jesus and the Bible."

I had heard yet another miraculous story of a Muslim becoming convinced of Jesus' true identity by means of a dream. It is confusing and difficult for a Muslim to be convinced by intellectual proofs, so the Holy Spirit often speaks to them of His existence and power through dreams. Most Muslims need a supernatural confirmation before they take that enormous iconoclastic step of faith to transfer their allegiance from the Qur'an and Mohammed to Jesus Christ and the Bible. ("The King's Gift" at the end of this book will further clarify the journey a Muslim woman most likely will travel before she surrenders her life to Christ.)

While many Muslims searching for truth have dreams of Jesus, such dreams should be understood primarily as a starting point. Some who have dreams give their lives to Jesus immediately, as Rania and Sabrina did. But not all do. Abdi, who dreamed of Jesus' waking him on Easter (see chapter 9), and Nasrin, who dreamed of the beautiful villas (see chapter 16), both had phenomenal dreams, but to this day I have not heard that either has accepted Jesus as their Savior. A convincing dream should not be equated with spiritual growth, and they do not usually sustain or preserve a person long-term. Dreams confirm, convince or persuade the seeker, but daily study of the Word of God produces growth.

"I want to give you a gift, Joy," Rania said after her baptism, handing me a long, soft red scarf. "I like the color red because it reminds me of the blood of Jesus shed on the cross for me. His blood is precious to me."

Taking the red scarf in my hands, I choked up. What a precious gift to receive! "Thank you, Rania. I will always treasure this because of what it symbolizes," I whispered to her, hardly able to speak. We were both opening the gift of salvation together at that sacred moment.

Prior to her conversion Rania had obtained two expensive gems from a man considered to be a healer. It is common for Muslim women to be attached to and dependent upon charms such as these, which are believed to give them protection or ensure well-being. For years Rania had either worn them or carried them in her purse. She had never taken them into a bathroom because she had been told that room is unclean and not the appropriate place for a stone of protection. She believed in the stones' protective abilities and had developed a dependency on them. After her baptism, however, she became convicted by the Holy Spirit of this dependency and felt she should get rid of them. But taking this step was stressful for Rania. One Sunday afternoon my friend came over to our house and told us about a disturbing incident she had experienced. While passing by the stones in her room, she felt an eerie yanking at her ankle. Having a new, clearer understanding of the spiritual world and having been convicted of her dependency on these gems, she knew it was time to part with the gems. Together we walked out to the garbage bin, and I witnessed her throw the expensive gems into the trash—forever cutting her off spiritually from

She has been freed from the bondage of trying to measure up to Allah and other people and is enjoying the acceptance she has found in Jesus. I am honored to call her my sister in Christ.

them and freeing her from her dependency on them. She was now firmly planted in Jesus, her true Protector. It was a day of celebration and victory.

Today Rania is enjoying the gift of Jesus and exudes passion and certainty in Him. Her face now radiates with joy when she talks about the gift of Jesus. She has been freed from the bondage of trying to measure up to Allah and other people and is enjoying the acceptance she has found in Jesus. I am honored to call her my sister in Christ.

Muslim Conversion Can Take a Long Time

It never ceases to thrill me when I have the privilege of welcoming another precious sister into the Kingdom and witness her settling into her true home in Christ! It is possible, and it is happening. If we rise above our fear of Muslims and believe we can be at home with them in the Kingdom, then we will see amazing things happen. But if we remain in fear, staying away from them, then we will be deprived of seeing the glory of God at work. Their journey into the Kingdom and our journey to come alongside them normally takes a long time. It can take years for Muslims to process the new information and concepts of Christianity and to deal with the personal costs they inevitably will encounter. We must have perseverance and patience, as well as a willingness to battle in prayer for the spiritual veil to be removed from their eyes.

My sisters in Jesus and I have found our home in Jesus and in the Kingdom—and with each other. Praise God!

18

The Wedding Party

I was packed, ready to move to another city, when Malia called to say goodbye. Her voice was cracking with emotion as she sweetly and affectionately stated, "Joy, I just want to be wherever you are." I cried. I had grown quite fond of Malia.

"Malia, I want you to be with me, too, wherever I am—and that means in heaven, also," I answered. As far as I know, Malia is not in the Kingdom yet, although her heart is known only to our Creator. I pray for Malia. I pray we will be together in heaven.

Indeed, this is my heart's desire for all women from Muslim backgrounds. I desire that they put their faith in our strong Savior and come along with me to heaven. I pray they will join me on this pilgrimage—not a *Hajj* pilgrimage to Mecca or any other earthly place, but a journey homeward to heaven, the place where we will be fully satisfied and blessed forever, where we will share eternity together and with our precious Lord Jesus.

Weddings among Muslims

Young women all over the world dream of the exciting day when they will be married. Among Muslims, engagement and wedding parties are the biggest events of their lifetimes. Preparation and planning for these auspicious celebrations can go on for months and sometimes years, and the events often last for days. They usually require elaborate wardrobes of dazzling wedding clothes and expensive jewelry and buffets of tantalizing food.

> ***"Malia, I want you to be with me, too, wherever I am—and that means in heaven, also," I answered.***

You may recall my description in chapter 1 of Sima's engagement party. It was certainly no exception. The mountains of gold jewelry, the expensive perfumes wafting through the air, the fancy embroidered Arab caftans and gorgeous silk *shalwar kameez* suits, the perfectly plucked and formed eyebrows and beautifully accentuated dark eyes laden with shadow and liner, the mountains and mountains of mouthwatering Middle Eastern dishes that greeted the guests—all these characteristics are typical of a Muslim engagement or wedding celebration. And more than that, the anticipation of such celebrations fills a person with a sense of suspense and mystery.

Anticipating Our Wedding in Heaven

We Christians greatly anticipate another wedding party. It will be quite different from any Muslim celebration—or any other earthly celebration, for that matter—and it will be more magnificent than anything we have ever seen. Even now preparations are being made for this wedding party, which will be the biggest event to take place in all of history. I am talking about the wedding banquet that will occur in heaven at the end of the age.

Although much is unknown to us and remains a mystery, we do know who the main characters in this wedding will be. Scripture tells us that the Church, which includes people from every nation and tribe on earth who have put their faith in Jesus Christ, will be there dressed as the Bride. Spiritually speaking, we will be washed clean. Anointed in precious, sweet-smelling oils and wearing white robes and elaborate crowns on our heads, we will await our beloved Savior.

And who is this Savior? He is the One who has created the Way for us to be there. He is Jesus the Christ, who gave up everything for us so that we can spend eternity with Him in His glorious home.

It is important for Muslims to understand that this is not a literal wedding as we would think of one on earth between a man and a woman. The wedding in heaven is a figurative analogy that refers to the Church, "the Bride of Christ," finally being united with Jesus, our Savior, to live with Him forever. Whereas the "Paradise" described in the Qur'an is a place where Muslims believe they will be rewarded with physical and sensual pleasures, this is not at all the picture of heaven as described in the Bible. Rather, heaven is a place where Christian believers will spend eternity worshiping God in the fullest sense. The wedding feast is a feast of final, eternal union with our God.

One night while anticipating the joys and mysteries of heaven, I was transported through the eyes and ears of faith as I imagined heaven's culminating wedding party where Jesus and the global Church from all of history at last will be united eternally. I envisioned joining the immense crowd making its way into the wedding party, and I was overtaken by a great sense of excitement and suspense. The crowd began to speak together the words from Revelation 5:12: "Worthy is the Lamb who was slaughtered—to receive power and riches and wisdom and strength and honor and glory and blessing." As they spoke, their voices grew stronger in intensity and clarity.

And then as I entered the banquet hall, there He was! I had always pictured Him as a gentle shepherd, yet my Lord was dressed as a conquering warrior! The image of Jesus in the stained-glass window that had captured my attention that day in church long ago paled in comparison to the Warrior King I now saw before me in my mind's eye. I stared in disbelief at His robe, which had been dipped in blood, and at the banner attached to His thigh, which read in big bold letters, "King of kings and Lord of lords." The ornate crown on His head was dazzling with gold and jewels of every imaginable kind. *Could it be that many of those jewels represent my treasured sisters who have come out of Muslim backgrounds to follow and serve Him?* I thought.

Every eye was riveted on our majestic Warrior King, who took center stage. He walked to His magnificent throne and sat down, a movement that carried with it a triumphant finality. Overcome with wonder and awe, we collectively collapsed to our knees and lifted our hands in praise as we chanted in unison, "Blessing and honor and glory and power belong to the one sitting on the throne and to the Lamb forever and ever" (Revelation 5:13). We knew it was time for this Warrior King, who had endured such terrible dishonor on the cross and had been held up as a spectacle of the worst imaginable kind of shame, finally to receive the highest honors

Could it be that many of the jewels in the King's crown represent my treasured sisters who have come out of Muslim backgrounds to follow and serve Him?

of which He was so worthy. Each of us desired only to give Him all the honor and glory we could possibly give.

A wave of pride in my Savior welled up in me. His majesty and splendor took my breath away. He was so magnificent there in his red robe, crown and banner. I knew that no evil thing could exist in His presence. All curses, sorcery, witchcraft, evil spirits, evil eye schemes, accusers, liars and deceivers would die instantly if exposed to this pure, holy presence. And I knew in my innermost being that I could not be present here if it were not for my Jesus, who had removed my filthy clothes of sin and so lovingly clothed me with His righteousness.

The music began again, and we dared to stand. Jesus, the victorious Warrior King, beckoned for us to come close to Him. My sisters from Muslim backgrounds, whom I saw all around me, responded immediately to His invitation. They began to express their heartfelt worship in freedom and beauty. Without hesitation I joined them, reveling in the joy of the moment and dancing in pure, childlike abandonment. Gone was empty ritual. Hallelujah! My sisters were happy and free, and so was I. Knowing this joy would go on forever and ever thrilled us. Each of us was loved and felt no shame or fear. No longer prisoners of what had been our greatest fears on earth—the fear of being punished by God and the fear of hell—we exulted in the freedom of our Savior and the joy of being safe in heaven with Him. He had risen from the dead and conquered death, and He had the power to spare us from hell and bring us to heaven. The unfathomable, immense love of Jesus filled the entire heaven. What a glorious King!

My Sisters in Heaven

Heaven. Is there any more beautiful or captivating word? The word evokes a sense of completion, perfection, relief, triumph, joy, sweet reunion, surprise and incomparable beauty. The mystery of heaven remains as long as we are mortal. Yet because of Jesus' redemptive work on the cross, the mystery will be uncovered. We who believe in Him will experience heaven in all its beauty and glory. This is for certain, not *inshallah* ("if Allah wills").

I want to go there. Indeed, I greatly anticipate the day I will see Him face-to-face. But I do not want to go there alone. I want my friends from Muslim backgrounds to go there with me.

My daily prayer is that the Bride of Christ will include my precious friends from Afghanistan, Somalia, Tunisia, Morocco, Algeria, Kurdistan, Pakistan, Southeast Asian countries and many others. I want them to understand deep in their hearts that if it were up to our good deeds, as Muslims believe, we would never be allowed to enter Paradise. I want them to understand that we could never do enough good to measure up to God's perfect standard. I want them to know that it is only through Jesus Christ, who gave His life for each one of them, that the mystery of heaven will be unveiled. Yes, I want them to understand the unbelievable, painful cost that Jesus paid for them, and I want them to know the complete and utter abandonment of His love. I want them to be warmly welcomed with me by the open arms of our gentle Shepherd and Savior. I want them to be there with me as we look on His face for the first time, as we gaze at His glorified, healed scars from the cross and as we find some way to express our deepest gratitude for the way He removed the punishment we deserve. I want them to live in heaven with me and with Him forever.

In the preface to this book I described how I sat drinking tea one day with my friend Safia in her tastefully decorated living room when she asked, "Joy, just exactly what do you do?" I answered simply, "Safia, I help prepare people for the next life."

Indeed, this life is short. My heart is for my Muslim friends to be ready for the next life. My goal is to help them understand how knowing Jesus Christ can prepare them for death and eternity. I want to unfold for them the wonderful truths about *Isa al Masih*, as Jesus is referred to in the Qur'an, and to lead them to understand how they can be ready for their eternal home in heaven.

I wait for the day when my Muslim friends will find Jesus to be their home.

I wait for the day when my Muslim friends will find Jesus to be their home. I anticipate with great excitement the day when we will feel at home together in the Kingdom as sisters in Christ.

19

A Letter to the Muslim Reader

Dear Muslim reader,

Perhaps someone gave you this book. Perhaps you purchased it yourself. Either way, I am thrilled you have read it. Although it is written to a Christian audience, it is really for you.

You may be left, however, with questions or disturbing thoughts about the Good News of *Isa al Masih*. Do not be afraid to ask questions. God gives you permission to do so. My hope and prayer is that this book has given you a bit more clarity and a desire to know more about Jesus.

I once had a Caucasian friend whom I visited often. I would go to her house and knock on the door. Many times she would open the door and we would chat at the entrance. I wanted so much to be invited inside. You can imagine my feelings. In your culture this kind of response would be considered rude and unacceptable.

With other friends in my life, I have had to make an appointment to visit. I am welcomed into their homes, but I know that my visit has to suit them and fit their schedule.

But with some friends and family, the door is open at all times. No appointment is necessary. I can just visit whenever I want and stay as long as I want. Ah, now that feels like home!

In the same way, *Isa al Masih* comes to the door of each person's heart and knocks. We have a choice to make. We can choose not to open the door of our hearts and ignore His knocking. We can choose to open the door and chat at arm's length. Or we can choose to invite Him inside, mess and all.

He waits for you to invite Him inside. All you need to do is ask Him to come into your heart. You may be embarrassed by the sins that cause shame in your life. He can clean up the mess. Just ask Him to kindly do that, and He will. He wants to make His home within your heart. You are deeply loved and cherished by *Isa al Masih*.

I encourage you to obtain the Holy Bible from a bookstore or library, or to read it online. You may want to start by reading the part called the gospels (the *Injil*). The gospels include the books of Matthew, Mark, Luke and John. These books will give you the full story of *Isa al Masih*.

Ask God to show you the truth. He has promised to show us truth. The Holy Spirit will direct you step by step. May you enter into the joy of discovering that *Isa al Masih* has come to make His home in your life.

Will you be there at heaven's wedding party? I pray you will.

May God bless you, my friend.

In the love of Jesus Christ,
Joy

Appendix

The King's Gift

Once upon a time there lived a wise and benevolent king. Though all kinds of rare and exotic animals lived in his vast kingdom, the songbirds were his favorites. Each sang a unique melody that delighted the king. By royal decree, he had made it known that he would pay a dear price to acquire more songbirds for his estate.

One day, merchants from a caravan told the king about an exquisite bird with deep rose and turquoise plumage who sang the most enchanting song they had ever heard. But this bird lived in a faraway land, imprisoned in a delicately crafted golden cage that hung outside a tailor's shop. The wicked tailor struck her cage often in fits of anger. Frightened and confused, the poor little bird dared to sing only at night.

The king grew angry at hearing the story, and he was determined to rescue this helpless creature. So he commissioned his most trusted servant to find the bird and purchase it. The servant saddled a strong horse and prepared many provisions, for the journey would be long. He also took a large sack of gold coins, for the king was willing to pay a high price.

Weeks passed. Then on a warm spring day the king's servant returned, holding aloft the glittering cage with a triumphant smile. The journey had been quite difficult, and the tailor had demanded a high price indeed.

The king took the golden cage to a special place in the lush garden where he spent his evenings reveling in the great variety of songs the birds sang. In this garden he tenderly hung the golden cage, gazing with compassion at the frightened creature within.

He opened the cage's tiny door, leaving it ajar. Then he walked away, for the bird was fearful and struck her frail body against the sides of the cage again and again.

After some weeks had passed, and spring gave way to summer, the jewel-colored bird was no longer afraid. This garden was a place of peace. Her cage door was still open, and no one had harmed her. She was especially glad that no one beat her cage anymore.

Day after day she watched the gentle king as he strolled in the garden speaking to the birds and caressing them. They all responded in outbursts of song.

All the birds seemed so happy. They freely flew in and out of their cages, singing and chirping to the king for hours on end. Some of them were brightly hued; others were only a common brown. Some were young; others had streaks of gray in their feathers. Nevertheless, the king loved them equally, as if he did not even notice they all were different.

One sunny day a cheerful canary went to visit the beautiful bird in the golden cage. Flying in through the open door, she fluffed her feathers and settled herself on the swing. Soon the two birds were chatting about nearly everything. The canary admired the fancy feeding dish and mirror. She had never seen such luxury! The canary also told her new friend of the most wonderful privilege of all—eating grain from the king's own hand. But the lovely bird chose to eat alone in her cage.

They talked about the open door. The richly colored bird explained to the canary that even though she was curious about life in the garden, she really had no desire to venture out. Besides, her father and mother, her grandparents and many of her relatives had been born and raised in cages. To her, they all seemed to have happy and fulfilled lives.

The canary tried patiently to explain that the king was offering an invitation to leave the golden cage, as beautiful as it was. The lovely bird would be free to fly. And she could even eat choice grain from the king's hand. The canary reminded her that the king had paid a high price to bring her to his garden.

Day after day the king walked past, holding out his hand at the door of the golden cage. He yearned for the little bird to come to him, but she was still too frightened of the unknown to move beyond her swing and feeding dish. Being a perfect gentleman, the king would never force her to leave the home she had always known. He had simply opened the door, waiting patiently for her to decide to fly out on her own. The king longed for her to experience the true joy and peace of mind that awaited her.

Several years passed. The happy little canary continued to visit her beautiful friend often, cheering her up with news about happenings all over the kingdom. The imprisoned bird continued to preen and fluff her feathers, satisfied only with glimpses of the king.

And her small, golden door remained open.

—by Charlene R. Hoskins

Glossary

abaya—long covering cloak for religious Muslim women. It differs from the ***burqa***, which is more of a one-piece, tent-like covering used in Afghanistan and Pakistan.

Allah—Arabic word for God

Eid *(pronounced "Eed")*—religious celebration

Eid al Adha *(pronounced "Eed-el-UHD-ha")*—commemorating festivity of Abraham's willingness to sacrifice Ishmael, according to Muslim belief

Eid al Fitr *(pronounced "Eed-el-FIT-ter")*—celebration ending the month of fasting

Hajj—religious pilgrimage to Mecca, Saudi Arabia

halal—permissible according to Islamic law

haram—not permissible according to Islamic law

hijab *(pronounced "hee-JOB")*—Islamic headscarf for observant Muslim women

Injil—the gospel accounts of Jesus Christ written by Matthew, Mark, Luke and John

inshallah *(pronounced "in-SHAH-lah")*—"if Allah wills"

Isa al Masih *(pronounced "Eesa-el-MAH-si")*—Muslim name for Jesus Christ, or Jesus the Messiah

Islam—the religion of Muslims

jinn—good or bad supernatural beings made out of smokeless flames of fire

Ka'aba—House of Allah in Mecca, direction for prayer

Mohammed—the final prophet, according to Muslim belief

mosque—Muslim place of worship

Muslim—follower of Islam

nabi—prophet

Qur'an (or ***Koran***)—Muslims' holy book

Ramadan—obligatory month of fasting

Shahada—Muslim declaration: "There is no god but Allah, and Mohammed is the prophet of Allah."

About the Author

Most of her life, Joy Loewen has either lived or ministered among Muslims. She was born in Yemen of American missionary parents, the late Warren and Dorothy Modricker, who pioneered the Gospel to the Somali people living in Yemen, Somalia, Ethiopia, Kenya and United Arab Emirates. Ruth and Grace, a set of twins, were born in Yemen, with only Ruth surviving. Charlie (now deceased), Dan and Mary followed. Ten years later twins John and Joy were born.

Observing her mother's diligent work of giving the Somali people the Scriptures in their own language and her father's bold witness, even in the midst of danger, left indelible impressions on Joy. At nineteen she accompanied her father on an evangelistic trip to the Somali Ogaden area in Ethiopia. It was at that time that Joy sensed the Lord setting her apart for missionary service among Muslims.

After leaving her childhood home in Somalia, Joy attended Moody Bible Institute in Chicago, where she met her husband, Ed, from Canada. She now holds both American and Canadian citizenships. With two-year-old Christina, the Loewens went to Pakistan, where they ministered from 1978 to 1988 at a mission hospital in the rural Himalayan foothills, and where their son, Jonny, was born. It was there, sitting among the Pakistani patients at their bedside, that Joy came to love Muslim women and to understand how to communicate the love of Jesus to them.

From time to time the Loewens traveled from their rural setting to big cities, where they observed college students and began dreaming of connecting more with young Muslim adults. That longing never left Joy.

Her ten years in Pakistan prepared and led her to return to Canada to share the Good News of Jesus with Muslim university students, immigrants and refugees, many of whom have become her good friends. Over the past twenty years in ministry in Canada, Joy also has come alongside numerous women who have left Islam and are following Jesus Christ. She serves with a parachurch organization that reaches out to Muslims.

Joy desires to equip Christian women to understand how to befriend Muslim women and share the Gospel with them. Her equipping seminars have taken her to cities across Canada. She can be contacted at info@awmcanada.org.

She and her husband enjoy spending time with their two married children and five grandchildren. Joy is also an avid reader, particularly appreciating books on spiritual formation. It gives her great delight to make her home a sanctuary for herself and others.